S0-FJL-792

The Audience *in* the News

LEA's COMMUNICATION SERIES
Jennings Bryant/Dolf Zillmann, General Editors

Select titles in LEA's Communication series include:

Biocca/Levy • Communication in the Age of Virtual Reality

Gershon • The Transnational Media Corporation: Global Messages and Free Market Competition

Harris • Health and the New Media: Technologies Transforming Personal and Public Health

Vorderer/Wulff/Friedrichsen • Suspense: Conceptualizations, Theoretical Analysis, and Empirical Explorations

Weaver/Tamborini • Horror Films: Current Research on Audience Preferences and Reactions

For a complete list of other titles in LEA's Communication Series, please contact Lawrence Erlbaum Associates, Publishers.

The Audience *in* the News

Dwight DeWerth-Pallmeyer
*California Polytechnic State University,
San Luis Obispo*

LEA LAWRENCE ERLBAUM ASSOCIATES, PUBLISHERS
1997 Mahwah, New Jersey

Copyright © 1997 by Lawrence Erlbaum Associates, Inc.
All rights reserved. No part of this book may be repro-
duced in any form, by photostat, microfilm, retrieval
system, or any other means, without the prior written
permission of the publisher.

Lawrence Erlbaum Associates, Inc., Publishers
10 Industrial Avenue
Mahwah, New Jersey 07430

Cover design by Jessica LaPlaca

Library of Congress Cataloging-in-Publication Data

DeWerth-Pallmeyer, Dwight.
The Audience *in* the news / by Dwight DeWerth-Pallmeyer.
p.   cm.
Includes bibliographical references and indexes.
ISBN 0-8058-2110-4 (cloth). — ISBN 0-8058-2111-2
(pbk.)
1. News audiences.   I. Title.
PN4784.N48D48   1996
302.23—dc20   96-23826
                                                 CIP

Books published by Lawrence Erlbaum Associates are printed
on acid-free paper, and their bindings are chosen for strength
and durability.

Printed in the United States of America
10 9 8 7 6 5 4 3 2 1

To Amy

Contents

Acknowledgments

This book grew out of my professional experience as a radio news director and out of my academic interests in the role audience plays in the thinking and working of mass media professionals. Reflecting back on the research and the subsequent writing and clarification of the work, there are many to whom I owe enormous thanks.

First, I would be remiss not to recognize the immense help and impetus of James Ettema, Director of the Department of Communication Studies at Northwestern University. Jim did far more than simply read through my manuscript and offer a bit of reaction. He offered me clear direction and valuable input from the conception of the project through the completion. His advice was crucial in the development of the key ideas in the document, and he carefully helped me refine those ideas with helpful questions and further probes. Working with him demonstrated to me why he is so widely published and recognized in the field.

I also wish to thank other critical readers at Northwestern, James Webster and Paul Hirsch. The research of both men and their interpersonal relationships with me have been a source of inspiration. I'm also grateful to John Lavine and Mary L. Dedinzky with the Medill School of Journalism for their assistance in helping me secure research site locations.

I am very much indebted to the many employees of *The Chicago Tribune* and WGN-TV, who let me into their work lives and gave me their time and support. I also want to thank both *The Chicago*

Tribune and WGN-TV organizations for opening up their facilities for my research.

The chance to work with the Communications series editor for Lawrence Erlbaum Associates, Jennings Bryant, was a treat. Jennings' enthusiastic support for this project, from our first phone conversation to the most recent, was a real asset. I admire him both as an editor and as a communications scholar. I am also indebted to Acquisitions Editor Kathleen O'Malley and Production Editor Debra Ruel for their assistance in putting this project into book form.

Colleagues at several institutions offered helpful support. Nishan Havandjian, Randall Murray, and Harry Sharp at Cal Poly continue to be supportive of my research. I also thank my colleagues at Utica College of Syracuse University. First, I'm thankful to Dean Thomas Brown, and the college as a whole, for a summer grant that allowed me the time to turn this research into book form. I would especially like to thank the Associate Dean of the Humanities, Frank Bergmann who offered me enthusiastic support for my research and has been a real ally to me. Thanks also to my departmental colleagues David Habbel and Carol Downing and to my office mates, Marsha Basloe and Cecilia Friend.

I want to thank my colleagues formerly associated with Augustana College in Rock Island, Illinois who offered encouragement, particularly Dan Bozik and William Purcell. My thanks also to Dan Wackman at the University of Minnesota who was the first to encourage me to pursue communications research.

My family has been a special asset to me. Both the financial and emotional support of my parents was vital to enabling me to see my way through this research. Thanks, Mom and Dad! My special joy and inspiration has come from my wife, Amy, likely the biggest prize I received during my Chicago experience. As we pledged in our wedding vows, Amy is indeed my confidant and friend. She has also been a manuscript reader and typist. My love and thanks go to her. To that end, I also thank the Chicago Transit Authority, which enabled me to meet her one fine wintry day. My daughter, Rachel, has been such a joy for me and a great teacher in helping me rediscover what is really important in life, things like faith and hope and love. And I am thankful to Dog and Cat, for their saliva-filled licks of support.

Finally, I thank my God, whose grace always has been, continues to be, and always will be, sufficient for me.

Introduction:
How Audience Images Help
Construct the News

In recent years, communications scholars have taken a renewed interest in analyzing the audience and its impact on the communication process, for example, Ang (1991) in *Desperately Seeking the Audience,* Neuman (1991) in *The Future of the Mass Audience,* and Ettema and Whitney (1994c) in *Audiencemaking: Media Audiences as Industrial Process.* Similarly, news editors and producers have often turned toward a marketing orientation that seeks to give news readers and viewers what they want, or at least what they say they want. Yet, there still has been little written about just how the audience factors into the news that is produced. In this book, I seek to fill that niche. I argue that audience images are quite important in the construction of news, but are not easily detected. That is because journalists are not principally interested in their audience; they are interested in the news.

Traditionally, when media scholars have tried to describe the role audience members play in the construction of news texts, they have started by asking reporters their impression of audience members, and then gauged how accurate those journalists' impressions of the audience were when patterned against demographic data. Generally, the results were discouraging. Reporters did not seem to have an accurate impression of their audience. Journalists had understandings of their audience, but those understandings were varied and fragmented.

When the accuracy of journalists' descriptions of their audience is solely used to assess the role the audience plays in constructing the news text, the conclusion is that the impact is minimal.

In this book, I argue that although journalistic images of the audience may be "incomplete," they do exist and powerfully help shape the work of journalists in producing journalistic texts. Some have already argued that those images are important. Pool and Shulman (1959), for example, discovered that different impressions of the audience led to different levels of accuracy in written reports.

It is also misleading to argue that reporters do not "know" their audience simply because they are not keyed into demographic information about them. Much of what journalists know about their audience is not so easily defined. What they know about their audience is imbedded in their work routines and is not easily expressed. It is an example of tacit knowledge that Schön (1983) labeled *knowing-in-action* (pp. 53–54). When journalists argue about which stories ought to be covered, they are conveying a tacit understanding about their audience. They may not explicitly talk about their readers or viewers in their discussions, but understandings about them are clearly cornerstones of their argument.

What news workers see as their primary task is not understanding their audience, but creating their product: individual news stories or the newspaper or newscast as a whole. Therefore, their focus is on what Ryan and Peterson (1982) labeled *product image* (p. 25). Journalists are predominantly concerned with gathering information and crafting stories. It is within this context that one must consider their understanding of their audience. To probe journalists' perception of their audience, one should not rely exclusively on asking them about that audience, but should instead examine the product they produce. The newspaper and the newscast tell as much about journalists' understanding of their audience as do explicit questions about their readers or viewers.

Additionally, the images of the audience that exist in the minds of reporters is only one way in which the audience has a bearing on the news that is produced. Audience is also tacitly factored into the entire newsmaking process. It is factored into the entire makeup of the news organization and is also an institutional part of the structure within which the news organizations function.

For example, in her classic work *Making News,* Tuchman (1978) argued that organizational factors account for much of the news that is reported. Regularly covered areas, or *beats*, for example, allow for news to be reported regularly from some sites and ignored at others. However, one can further argue that news beats are set up on the tacit premise that the audience is particularly interested in certain topics or is especially affected by those areas. There is the built-in acknowledgment in the newsroom that audience members are particularly attracted to celebrities encountered in the Hollywood beat and are particularly affected by the goings-on at their local city hall. Impressions of the audience help shape the organizational plans that help guide news directors and editors-in-chief. Beats are built around tacit notions of the audience. Similarly, news factors tied to the audience, such as interest and impact, are elevated over those less closely associated with the audience, such as conflict and prominence. Notions of the audience help define what is to be considered newsworthy.

The institutional environment within which news organizations operate also conveys tacit assumptions about the audience that help shape the news product. For example, Webster and Phalen (1994) argued that the legal environment within which broadcast policy is cast poses different models of the broadcast audience. They argued that during the Reagan years, Federal Communications Commission (FCC) policy, which centered around deregulation of broadcasting, posed the broadcast audience as "consumer." Such a policy, which eventually led to the abandonment of the Fairness Doctrine and other broadcast obligations, led many radio stations to abandon most of their local news operations because they were not earning the stations profits—presumably because news did not adequately appeal to the broadcast consumer.

Organizational structures and institutional arrangements are imbedded with images of the audience that do help shape the style and kinds of news that are produced.

The key arguments presented in this book are illustrated using a case study of news workers and news texts at two Chicago newsgathering organizations, *The Chicago Tribune* and WGN-TV. Both are owned by the Tribune Company, a media giant based in Chicago. In chapter 1, I examine notions of audience and how they have been treated by academicians. I review audience image as conceptualized at three levels of analysis: the individual, the organizational, and the institutional. I then introduce the argument that perceptions of the audience help shape the news product within news organizations.

In chapter 2, I present a detailed description of the ways in which audience is imbedded within the news construction process. I develop that understanding by laying out three central arguments: (a) news is the result of practical accomplishment; (b) journalists predominantly know and concern themselves with product image; and (c) although journalists work with no formalized audience image, a tacit image of the audience does develop out of the journalists' work with the product (news stories, newscasts, newspapers).

In chapters 3 and 4, I present a very representative set of journalistic news values. In chapter 3, I examine notions of audience within the news values of *timeliness, proximity, conflict,* and *prominence:* factors that appear inherently less closely linked to audience concerns. In chapter 4, I address the news values of *impact* and *interest,* factors that are more closely linked to audience. I also show how those two news values are linked to journalists' impressions of what are important stories. The key question underlying both of these chapters is "How are notions of audience imbedded in these news values?"

In chapter 5, I present differing ideas of audience at three key levels of the news organizations: reporters and news gatherers; editors and producers; and senior editors, producers, and news directors. In this chapter, I also offer some detail about how news workers learn about their audiences.

In the conclusion, chapter 6, I seek to summarize and position this study within the larger body of mass communication research. I address the following concerns:

- A greater understanding of the working theories of audience within news organizations. Particular attention is paid to the wide range of images used to represent the audience and the subtle way those images are imbedded into the newsmaking process.
- An explanation of why audience images do not fit neatly into any standard news model.
- A greater understanding of the modern news product and how audience concerns help shape the definition of news.
- A picture of what journalists' deem to be their best work: stories that impact their audience in a special way. In this chapter I argue that, ultimately, journalists are seeking ways to touch their audience and make their writing empathetic.

Chapter 1

The News Audience in Theory

In this society, the overwhelming majority of print, broadcast, and visual media fulfill their social responsibilities only when they reach audiences which are themselves willing to pay for the media product or which are attractive enough to advertisers that they will pay the bills. In either case, the marketing perspective underscores the fact that audience members' preferences must be understood and taken into serious account as the media product is planned, developed, promoted, produced, and distributed. (Lavine & Wackman, 1988, p. 255)

A marketing perspective in modern news organizations presupposes that *audience* must be factored into the news production formula. Even for news workers and organizations that are not committed to a marketing orientation, audience is still a key consideration, albeit often tacitly factored into news judgments, technologies, and procedures. Perceptions of the audience are part of the overall construction of news.

In this book, I examine the impact notions of the audience have in constructing the news within news organizations. Specifically, I focus on the way different perceptions of audience are built into the news product as part of a product image and how those tacit and explicit understandings of the audience then help construct the news.

The argument I present in this book is that news workers are primarily concerned with creating the news product: stories, newscasts, or newspapers. Their objective is to *make* the best news they can. Though they do have real images of their audience, those images

1

are varied and fragmented. Much of news workers' understandings about their audience are bound up within product image and are, therefore, an example of tacit professional knowledge (Schön, 1983). Although such knowledge is often difficult to articulate, it is very real and does help shape the news product throughout the news organization.

Thus, we can best study the role the audience plays in the news construction process by looking at the news product itself and at journalists' rhetoric about their product, for understandings about the audience are imbedded within the product image.

To address this issue, it is useful to place this research within the context of the sociology of journalism, or what Schudson (1989) referred to as *the sociology of news production*. From that perspective, one presumes that news is a product flowing out of the interactions among workers within news organizations. One important source of that social construction among news workers and news organizations are images of the audience. In this chapter, I examine audience imagery within news construction at three levels of analysis: the individual, the organizational, and the institutional. I conclude this chapter by outlining the method used in this study. In the next chapter, I continue by outlining the specific focus of this book: how perceptions of audience help shape the news product within the news organization.

AUDIENCE IMAGES

Notions of the audience are clearly imbedded in newsmaking and can be clarified by examining audience from different levels of analysis. On the individual level, a variety of mass communications researchers (Darnton 1990; Gaunt 1990; Schlesinger 1978) argued that journalists do not really know their audiences. Schlesinger (1978) argued that "total audience remains an abstraction, made real on occasion by letters or telephone calls, encounters of a random kind in public places, or perhaps more structured ones such as conversations with liftmen, barmen and taxi-drivers" (p. 107).

Darnton (1990) recalled his days working on *The New York Times* and described the view of audience his staff used. Reporters were all to conceive of their audience as a 12-year-old girl. Darnton wrote that he came to question the use of this imaginary figure. He would ask himself, "What does a 12-year-old girl know about slum clearance in the South Bronx?" He said he later came to the conclusion that the 12-year-old girl really only existed in the folklore of 43rd Street. He concluded that his real audience consisted of other reporters in the *Times* newsroom. Others have argued that same point. They say that the journalist really doesn't concern himself or herself with the real readers of the paper. For example, in their study of Madison, Wisconsin, newspaper reporters, Flegel and Chaffee (1971) concluded that the reporters' perceptions of their readers' viewpoints had a low correlation with the viewpoints represented in their stories.

Still, journalists clearly do have some working sense of their audience, whether accurate or not. In White's (1950) "Gate Keeper" study, the newspaper editor he studied offered this description of his audience:

> Our readers are looked upon as people with average intelligence and with a variety of interests and abilities ... I see them as human and with some common interests. I believe they are all entitled to news that pleases them ... and news that informs them. (p. 390)

In their study, Pool and Shulman (1959) concluded that audience has a clear impact on the journalistic product: "The audience, or at least those audience about whom the communicator thinks ... play more than a passive role in communication" (p. 145). The authors' study concluded that "good news" stories tended to elicit views of the audience as supportive, while "bad news" stories led journalists to perceive of their audience as critics. When the student journalists who were studied had perceptions of a supportive audience, their "good news" stories were more accurate, and when they had perceptions of a critical audience, their "bad news" stories were more accurate.

In a factor analysis to determine which elements were influential in helping individual journalists judge what was newsworthy, Weaver and Wilhoit (1986) found journalists' impressions of audience research and their news sources to be a key factor. More recently, in a survey of editors from 540 newspapers in the United States, Chang and Kraus (1990) found that editors nationwide have strong perceptions of readers' interest in different news categories that are almost opposite of the editors' own stated interests.

Gans (1979), on the other hand, argued that journalists see the audience as something like themselves and therefore view themselves as audience representative: "Most journalists take the congruence of their own and the audience's feelings for granted. In the process they become representatives of the audience, reacting for it vis-á-vis their sources" (p. 237).

Accurate or not, individual journalists do have perceptions of their audience that help shape their work. Notions of the audience are also built into the workings of news organizations. Those who study news construction from the organizational level of analysis see that notions of the audience are imbedded within organizational routines and practices. Just as analysts approaching news from the organizational level have argued that the news product is a social construction, they might further argue that audiences, too, can be a social construction. As such, "audience" is used by journalists to convince their editors of a story's merit and used by organizations to sell to advertisers. From this perspective, working images of the audience are shaped to meet organizational needs. Those same audience images become imbedded in organizational practice.

In *Making News*, Tuchman (1978) argued that news organizations assume that audiences are interested in whatever they cover: "Today's news media place reporters at legitimated institutions where stories supposedly appealing to contemporary news consumers may be expected to be found" (p. 21).

While Tuchman might argue that audiences are assumed to be interested so as to meet the needs of the news organization, modern journalism practitioners argue that news organizations must do a better job of catering to audience tastes. Stone (1987), for example, contended that the modern editor must be concerned that each inch of journalism copy do its job of attracting and maintaining an audience. Indeed, the modern thrust of many news organizations seems to be a desire to grab their audiences and cater to them. In this sense, the audience is treated as a market to be captured. Obvious examples are the stylistic standards employed by Gannett Company newspapers and modern "infotainment" shows which consistently use sensationalistic tactics to attract their audience. The papers modeled after *USA Today* use flashy graphics, short copy, and so forth. Contemporary infotainment shows use a variety of "teases" to grab their viewers. Given the decline in newspaper readership and network viewership figures in the past decade, the current organizational perspective on the audience most commonly views the audience as a market to be captured to meet the revenue goals of the news organization.

That view of *audience as market* serving the news industry is also evidenced at the institutional level of analysis. Hackett (1984) summarized the institutional view this way:

Instead, we would analyze the various types of systematic orientations and relationships which unavoidably structure news accounts. These factors may indeed include partisan favoritism or political prejudices. But they also include criteria of newsworthiness, the technological characteristics of each news medium, the logistics of news production, budgetary constraints, legal inhibitions, the availability of information from sources, the need to tell stories intelligibly and entertainingly to an intended audience, the need to package news in a way which is compatible with the commercial imperative of selling audiences to advertisers and the forms of appearance of social and political events. All these factors and others shape the media's functioning as an ideological institution. (p. 269)

Thus, when journalistic audiences are examined from an institutional perspective, one considers regulatory and political factors, technological capabilities, economic pressures, and so forth, in relation to the news environment. Each factor, in turn, helps shape a unique image of the audience.

The seminal analysis of media systems authored by Siebert, Peterson, and Schramm, in *Four Theories of the Press* (1956), suggested that the shape of the media was inextricably bound to the social controls in the society. They suggested that four types of press systems had developed in modern societies: authoritarian, libertarian, social responsibility, and Soviet–Communist. Each theory also envisioned audience in a different way. For example, the authoritarian system envisioned knowledge as coming from a wise few. The audience was viewed as ignorant and so was given only the information that would be appropriate for them. The libertarian model grew out of the period of the enlightenment and therefore viewed the audience as, indeed, enlightened. Journalism was to work on behalf of the people, and to act as a watchdog against government. The social responsibility model suggested that the press had an obligation to provide the public with a forum that voiced a variety of competing ideas. As evidenced in early FCC policy, audience was viewed as an active democracy, requiring certain information. Last, the Soviet–Communist model portrayed the press as the servant of the state. The audience was viewed as "evolving" and maturing into a classless society.

Recent analyses suggest that modern journalists tend to embrace libertarian ideals (Akhavan-Majid & Wolf, 1991; Wuliger, 1991). Miller (1992) suggested that the same is true of news audiences: "There is overwhelming evidence people value the watch-dog role of the media. They definitely want us to keep an eye on public officials, to tell them when things are going wrong." Yet, arguing from an institutional point of view, Akhavan-Majid and Wolf (1991) said that American journalism actually consists of an elite-power group and so bypasses the audience. Hallin (1992), too, saw the press as political "insiders, too close to the powerful institutions whose actions need to be discussed" (p. 20).

The regulatory environment within U.S. broadcasting also shapes the broadcast journalism product and poses particular pictures of the audience. For example, in their analysis of broadcast policy, Webster and Phalen (1994) suggested that three, sometimes conflicting, models of audience have been represented. The first they called the *Effects Model, Audience as Victim*. This policy was perhaps best represented in former FCC Chairman Newton Minow's "Vast Wasteland" speech (1961). His message suggested that the audience must be protected from harmful media content or provided with healthier content. The second was called the *Marketplace Model, Audience as Consumer*. This policy was perhaps best voiced by the FCC chairman during the Reagan administration, Mark Fowler. The audience in this view was treated as active and knowledgeable, and the best media content, it was thought, would survive because it best catered to that audience. The third was called the *Commodity Model, Audience as Coin of Exchange*. This was the view evidenced in the 1979 FCC document on the deregulation of radio. In this legal scenario, audience was treated as an "object" for advertisers. The best media content was that which attracted a sizable audience that could be sold to advertisers.

Modern assumptions about the technologies available to news practitioners also convey assumptions about the news production process and the way in which the audience retrieves the news. One modern portrayal of the news audience from those who focus on the changing technological picture of news production is the audience as "technocrats" with a host of technological tools at their disposal to help them design the news for themselves. Generally, however, these images of the audience are a bit inflated because actual usage of these news products is less than expected by media visionaries. A second theory casts the audience as passive. Neuman (1991) contrasted the technocrat image of the audience with a passive, slow-moving audience. Although the technology for vast changes in the use of the media is possible, Neuman contended that those changes will be slow in coming because people are relatively passive when it comes to making changes in their private use of the media and because of economic constraints on the media themselves. His view suggests that changes within the news industry will also logically be slower in reacting to that passive audience.

A hybrid of these two views—audience as technocrat and audience as passive—is, again, implicitly *audience as market*. This is the view of large media organizations that are increasingly using new technologies to segment and personalize their materials for a variety of audiences. Smith (1992) began to view the audience from a market perspective in his recommendations to journalists and their news organizations:

> Why can't newspapers give readers what they want and what they need? Or give them what they need in a way that they can use it? I believe in the classic traditions of newspapers: Protecting the public's interest, ferreting out truth, and nailing scoundrels. That's why many of us got into newspapers, but whose interest is served if the newspaper is unread? (p. 34).

As a focus on segmenting audiences suggests, the newsgathering process has also been examined from an economic perspective. Economic models of the audience as devised by media economists such as Owen and Wildman (1992) typically treat the audience as rational. Audiences have clear preferences and will choose media content based on those preferences. These economists also characterize media organizations as completely rational entities that are operating exclusively to maximize profit. Squires (1993) suggested that such a view is increasingly practiced at modern news organizations like the Tribune Company:

> Owners and managers of the new media ... want content defined in advance by target audience responses to surveyor's questions and then designed to fit inside the elite and narrow parameters of the most desired advertiser targets with a single goal—attainment of the corporation's financial objectives. (p. 145)

As such an economic view implies, the institutional perspective of the audience as market goes beyond merely viewing the audience in terms of segmented groups, but instead "creates" an audience to meet the news organizations' needs within the institutional environment. Ettema and Whitney (1994a) argued, "In an institutional conception, actual receivers are ... reconstituted ... as institutionally effective audiences that have social meaning and/or economic value within the system" (p. 5). From the institutional perspective, the audience is viewed as a market served up for advertisers. The news organization looks to construct the best audience it can.

Overall, it is clear that a variety of ideas regarding audience are reflected among the different levels of analysis.

THE IMPLICIT AUDIENCE BEHIND WORKING THEORIES

McQuail (1983) distinguished between three types of theories at work in understanding the media: common-sense, working, and social-scientific theories. *Common-sense* theories are those that develop out of media usage by everyday media consumers. McQuail argued that these theories are important because they are often reflected in public opinion polls and help shape public policy toward the media. *Working* theories are those understandings that tend to govern and guide the behavior of media professionals. *Social-scientific* theories are, of course, those created within the academic environment.

Because the focus of this research is on how views of the audience bear on the construction of news within organizations, the theories of the audience most relevant for study are working theories. News workers at both of the news organizations I observed (WGN-TV and the *Chicago Tribune),* are quoted at length to illustrate these working theories.

Images of the audience, like other journalistic working theories, develop out of the everyday work of the journalist. In his text, *The Reflective Practitioner,* Schön (1993) described working professionals as those who must "deliberately involve themselves in messy but crucially important problems and, when asked to describe their methods of inquiry, they speak of experience, trial and error, intuition, and muddling through" (p. 43).

Such a depiction can be applied to journalists in their creation of news. Formal scientific theories are rarely used in the work process for the journalist, but working theories are used. Ettema (1988) applied Schön's model to the work of investigative journalists. Ettema argued that these journalists often operate intuitively in finding and defining news stories. Schön (1983) contended that professionals learn to do their job, based on past experience, although they might find it hard to verbalize:

When we go about the spontaneous, intuitive performance of the actions of everyday life, we show ourselves to be knowledgeable in a special way. Often we cannot say what it is that we know. When we try to describe it, we find ourselves at a loss, or we produce descriptions that are obviously inappropriate. Our knowing is ordinarily tacit, implicit in our patterns of action and in our feel for the stuff with which we are dealing. It seems right to say that our knowing is in our action.

Similarly, the workaday life of the professional depends on tacit knowing-in-action. (p. 49)

Such knowledge may also be applied to journalists' understanding of their audience. As the work of Darnton (1990), Gans (1979), Gaunt (1990) and Schlesinger (1978) indicates, journalists may not be able to clearly verbalize what they know, yet they may know, or at least intuit, a great deal. One can gain a little of that knowledge by listening to a journalist reflect on the creation of a story. Ettema (1988) recounted *Boston Globe* reporter Jonathan Kaufman's description of his doing a story on racial job discrimination in Boston:

Everyone knew Boston had problems with race relations, but the only way you'd be able to convince people was by actually documenting them. Anecdotes weren't going to get you anywhere because everybody had competing anecdotes. For every black guy you had being discriminated against, some white guy had a black guy who'd taken a job from him. It just didn't advance the argument at all.

My background as a *Globe* reporter had been a lot of street reporting, a lot of neighborhood reporting. I was always right out in the neighborhoods writing stories and one of the things you'd always hear in the white neighborhoods of this city was "The *Globe* is fulla shit ... The *Globe* is too liberal ... I don't trust the *Globe* ... My dog pisses on the *Globe*."

I thought for this to be useful, we have to get people to read it [but] how would you get people to read about an issue they were sick of reading about?

I remember talking to a reporter in the newsroom about it ... and he said, "Well, the best way to do it would be to go after Tip O'Neil, Harvard or the Bank of Boston." (pp. 32–33)

Such an account illustrates a good deal of the tacit knowledge this reporter had of his audience, although that was not the essence of his account. He was telling about how a story had developed, not who constituted his audience. In the reporter's first sentence he implies that his readers are basically knowledgeable about their immediate world but are skeptical enough to require proof for what they read. In the second paragraph cited, the reporter shows awareness of how his paper is viewed in differing neighborhoods of the city. He also illustrates one way in which he explicitly learns about his audience—from talk he hears on the streets. The last two paragraphs illustrate that tacit assumptions about the audience can lead to elevation of the news criterion of prominence. The reporter learns from a colleague that the only way to interest his audience is by citing a prominent source or institution.

This tacit knowledge forms a kind of working theory that Schön labeled *knowing-in-action*. By this, Schön meant knowledge that is used in performing a task without conscious deliberation. Schön structured such notions based on Polanyi's (1966) depiction of *tacit knowledge*—the idea that much of what we know is understood on a subconscious level, and is therefore, not easily described. Tacit knowledge applies to journalists and their perceptions of audience. The audience is not the key point of focus for the journalist; the story or news product as a whole is. Although perceptions of the audience are, of course, part of the journalist's knowledge base, these perceptions are often mediated by or organized within what Ryan and Peterson (1982) called *product image*.

This framework implies that a successful media product will usually be fashioned in such a way as to resemble past successes. The ultimate goal is to please decision makers at the next level in the chain of command. Specifically, a focus on product image is flexible enough so that the practitioners can mold their product to be most like the most successful products of the recent past. In news theory, this implies that reporters will likely fashion their stories to resemble the structure of the story that was last considered a "standout" story by their editor. The news producer will seek to organize newscasts in the same way that newscasts are traditionally organized. Page layout will likely follow "successful" styles.

When one applies this product-image framework to the decisions made within news organizations, one focuses on the news product for clues as to assumptions made about audience. Working theories of the news audience are often implicit or tacit within notions of product image. They are part of news workers' knowing-in-action as they create the news.

Espinosa (1982) hinted at this relation between product and audience in his ethnographic examination of a Hollywood producers' meeting on the creation of a television show: "Producers' perceptions of the audience are an important element in the construction of the television text ... producers have a perception of the audience which they employ to assess whether or not to include particular elements in their story" (p. 84). For Espinosa's producers, audience is not the explicit concern—the story is the obvious concern. Perceptions of the audience are indeed involved in the construction of the story, but they are imbedded within a discussion of the rules for good script writing. The title of Espinosa's article conveys such an interpretation: "The Audience in the Text ...."

If one similarly assumes that the story, newscast, or newspaper is the key concern for the news worker, one must also consider the values inherent in that product image to discover how more subtle audience imagery plays a part in the construction of news. Although researchers have suggested that standardized news values do little to actually identify what constitutes the news (Dimmick, 1974; Ettema & Whitney, 1994b), those news values are still a very real part of journalistic training and folklore, and hence, a very real part of the working theory behind news construction. Previously, there has been little study of the implicit understandings of audience (working theories) that operate within the tenets of commonly accepted news values.

In traditional textbook fashion, Itule and Anderson's *News Writing and Reporting for Today's Media* (1987) laid out the criteria by which journalists are trained to "identify" news and distinguish news from all other happenings:

- Timeliness: Is it a recent development or is it old news?
- Proximity: Is the story relevant to local readers?
- Conflict: Is the issue developing, has it been resolved or does anybody care?
- Eminence or prominence: Are noteworthy people involved? If so, that makes the story more important.
- Consequence or impact: What effect will the story have on readers?
- Human interest: Even though it might not be an earth-shattering event, does it contain unique, interesting elements? (p. 39)

Within each of these news values, there is imbedded an implicit understanding, if not a working theory, of the news audience. For example, Kaniss (1991) focused on the audience implicit in the news value of impact:

News directors often push reporters covering government plans or policies to "humanize" their stories. One television reporter described the instructions of her news director as she went out to cover the press conference of a city official announcing a proposal for a major capital investment: "We don't want facts and figures for the story. We want to humanize it." Another reporter commented, "The operative principle we think about all the time is people, people, people. If I'm telling you a tax story that's kind of dry and boring, I want to tell how it's going to affect you." (p. 120)

In Kaniss' discussion, audience almost translates into a news value itself. One prominent text, *News Reporting and Writing* (1988), written by faculty members at the University of Missouri School of Journalism (Brooks, Kennedy, Moen, & Ranley, 1988) goes so far as to list audience as the first criterion of newsworthiness: "The audience is the backdrop against which reporters and editors consider questions of news value" (p. 5). Although these authors treated audience as an explicit news value in itself, they did not explicate the underlying assumptions about audience that are imbedded in the other news values. For example, when discussing the notion of prominence as a news value they wrote, "Most people are interested in the private lives of public figures" (p. 13). They did not address why people have this fascination or why journalists believe people have this fascination. But that is the nature of a working theory as opposed to a social scientific theory: practical guidance without elaborate explanation.

There are also implicit understandings about the audience imbedded in other decisions related to the construction of news. For example, the need to make stories visually appealing in both print and television suggests a certain passivity of the news audience and a recognition by the news organization that the reader or viewer must be enticed to pay attention. Also, the everyday routines of news workers are imbedded with notions of the audience. For example, radio news reporters who regularly monitor other local radio newscasts in their market in the hour prior to their own next newscast may work hard to confirm any story the competitor has so they can legitimately use that story in their own next newscast. Such a procedure suggests that their news audience is more concerned with the latest-breaking details or greatest number of stories rather than with thoughtful analysis about "older" news.

News is the product of the everyday routines and tasks conducted by those working within news organizations. Imbedded in those routines are working images of the audience. They are a part of Schön's (1983) knowing-in-action.

METHOD

My focus in this book is to examine how explicit and tacit working theories of the audience help shape the news product among individual journalists and within the news organizations for which they work. A case study of the newsrooms at the *Chicago Tribune* and at WGN-TV is principally used to illustrate these concepts. Semistructured interviews were conducted with newsroom personnel over a 6-month period, from October 1992 through March 1993. In addition, several informal interviews were conducted during field observations at both sites. General information provided in this book about the news organizations, such as staff members, reflect the primary study period of October 1992 through March 1993.

Although this study includes examination of the whole news effort at WGN, special attention is focused on the noon newscast at the station. At the *Chicago Tribune,* attention is primarily focused on the reporting and editing by the city's metro desk.

Both WGN-TV and the *Chicago Tribune* are owned by the Chicago-based Tribune Company. Tribune is a media empire that owns six daily newspapers, seven independent television stations, six radio stations, and the Chicago Cubs baseball team. The company also has an interest in one of Canada's largest newsprint manufacturers and produces and syndicates both television and radio programming. In addition, the company started a cable news service on two Chicago cable systems on January 1, 1993, called *Chicagoland.* The WGN newscasts are aired on *Chicagoland* on a tape-delayed basis.

Based on its annual statement, the Tribune empire was worth more than $2.75 billion in 1992. Tribune earned $1.2 billion in operating revenues from its newspapers in 1992, and the Chicago Tribune accounted for 53% of that total. The company's seven television stations garnered $477 million in operating revenues in 1992.

WGN-TV, channel 9, airs 14 hours of local news each week. Its two main newscasts of the day air for 1 hour each at noon and at 9:00 p.m. WGN-TV is the only broadcast station in the Chicago market to air a noon newscast, although the ABC station, WLS-TV airs a half-hour newscast at 11:30 a.m. At 9:00 p.m., WGN-TV runs a newscast against one other independent station, WFLD-TV, channel 32. In 1992, WGN-TV also began airing a weekend morning news program. In addition to its local broadcast, WGN programming is carried on many cable systems throughout the country, enabling its newscasts to reach 40% of all U.S. households.

The news department at WGN-TV employs 58 full-time employees and 6 part-time employees, which is roughly half the size of each of the network-owned-and-operated stations in Chicago. The department is headed by a news director, Paul Davis, and an assistant news director, Jim Disch. The station employs seven general assignment reporters, three anchorpersons, two weathermen, and five sports reporters. Each newscast is headed by a producer, and there are also two executive producers of the news shows.

In comparison with the WGN-TV news department, the *Chicago Tribune* is far more complex, organizationally. The newsroom is headed by the managing editor, Dick Ciccone, to whom reports one deputy managing editor, Ann Marie Lipinski, and six associate managing editors. Reporting to Lipinski are four associate metro-politan editors, one who oversees city coverage, another who oversees suburban coverage, and two other editors who oversee the 13 copy editors and administrative matters.

Chicago Bureau Chief Jean Davidson (the city desk day editor) typically reports to Lipinski as well. Although lines of demarcation are blurred, 44 reporters are answerable to the city desk editors. Among them are five investigative reporters, who tend to work at their own pace. Whereas there are 44 reporters assigned to cover Chicago, there are 47 other reporters who are assigned to the four suburban bureaus.

The paper is primarily a morning-delivered newspaper with street sales, but there are five editions that are published daily including: the Midwest Edition, the Home Delivery Edition, the Sports Final, the Chicago Sports Final, and the Evening Wrap.

The daily paper is typically divided into six sections. These include the front page section, a local/metropolitan section, a business section, a sports section, a lifestyles section (called "Tempo"), and a special daily section. For example, featured on Tuesday is a section for children called "Kid News," and on Wednesday a section devoted to food is featured.

The paper is zoned. In 1992, the *Chicago Tribune* added a fifth major zoned edition serving Lake County, to the north of Chicago. In September 1992, the single issue price increased from $.35 to $.50 a copy, triggering a circulation decline. Still, the *Tribune* clearly is the dominant newspaper in the market.

There were several advantages stemming from the selection of WGN-TV and the Chicago-Tribune in this study. First, it is theorized that different conceptions of audience are found at different organ-izational levels. Therefore, the best chance for discovering different images of audience would be found in organizations with great organizational size and depth.

Second, interesting comparisons could be made between broad-casting and newspaper organizations. Numerous technological and economic changes have had an affect on both types of organizations leading to interesting questions. For example, has the advent of cable and declining network shares led to more of a market orientation toward audience in broadcasting over the past few years? Similarly, has the growth of a *USA Today* mentality changed conceptions of audience for the modern newspaper? In what ways are views of audience different among these two types of news operations?

Third, the most sophisticated news products and the most sophisticated models of audience are likely evidenced in major market settings. Typically, much of a major market mentality is passed along to smaller markets and, therefore, helps to shape those products. For example, it is far more likely that smaller papers in a chain will pattern themselves after the largest paper than vice versa.

CONCLUSION

What news workers see as their primary task is creating a product: individual news stories or the newspaper or newscast as a whole. Therefore, their focus is on what Ryan and Peterson (1982) labeled *product image*. Journalists are predominantly concerned with gathering information and crafting stories. If that is true, it is a mistake to understand the influence of the audience as simply represented by how accurate a journalist's understanding is of demographic information about his or her audience. Simple models of communication imply that the extent of audience input into the journalistic product lies in a direct relation between audience and journalist. They suggest that journalists learn about the audience, either directly from audience members (phone calls, letters to the editor, talk on the street) or from within the news organization, which has presumably engaged in formal audience analyses—ratings, readership studies, focus groups, and so forth. However, on a day-to-day basis, journalists typically have little time to seriously ponder how well they are communicating with an audience. Therefore, journalists do not readily voice a formal theory or detailed information about their audience. Their knowledge of audience is an example of Schön's (1983) *knowing-in-action*.

Both implicit and explicit understandings of the audience are an important consideration in the construction of news texts. Journalists work with no formal theory of audience but a variety of understandings about their audience developed through a variety of journalistic activities do make a powerful impact on shaping the news. In the following chapter, examples from WGN-TV and the *Chicago Tribune* are used to illustrate how tacit images of the audience develop out of journalists' focus on their news product in "accomplishing" the news.

Chapter 2

The Tacit Audience in Newsmaking

Those who research the sociology of journalism maintain that the news is not just something that happens in a void to be reported by journalists, but instead the news is something that is created by journalists from a myriad of happenings in and around their world. News, then, is constructed within the everyday work of journalists and within the organizations for which they are employed. In that process of constructing the news, various images of the audience evolve and further contribute to the kind of news that is produced.

In this chapter, examples from both WGN-TV and *The Chicago Tribune* are used to demonstrate three central notions: (a) News is the result of practical accomplishment, therefore, (b) journalists predominantly know and concern themselves with product image, and (c) although journalists work with no formalized audience image, a tacit image of the audience does develop out of the journalists' work with the product (news stories, newscasts, newspapers). These implicit notions of the audience have an impact on the news that is produced. Therefore, these notions are an example of Schön's knowing-in-action.

ILLUSTRATIONS OF PRACTICAL ACCOMPLISHMENT

Media scholars often talk about journalistic activity in language something akin to a manufacturing vocabulary. That is illustrated by the titles of some of the key texts that have focused on news gathering: *Making News* (Tuchman, 1978), *Making News* (Mayer, 1993), *Making Local News* (Kaniss, 1991), and *Manufacturing the News* (Fishman, 1980). That same manufacturing metaphor is shared by working journalists when asked to describe their work. For example, WGN Producer Tim Jackson describes his duties this way: "This is very much of a factory orientation ... what we do is not always brain surgery here. Sometimes we're paid to be analytical generalists, but an awful lot of the time we're doing a line job." By this, Jackson suggests that much of his work is performed quickly and relatively efficiently, with each employee completing their assigned tasks as in an assembly line. Similarly, WGN reporter Roseann Tellez implies that her job is to crank out the news product:

> We come in the morning and we're expected to have a story that night. And usually, in a city like Chicago ... there are so many stories that it's generally a matter of which ones do we want to rule out. So it's not a big problem for us all to turn out a story each day.

The reporter treats the stories as the commodity of her trade. Her language, "turn out a story each day," connotes a manufacturing metaphor. Deadline pressure forces the journalist to narrow her focus to the immediate job at hand—cranking out the news story. *Tribune* reporter Steve Johnson also uses language that casts the news story as a product that fills a need when he says:

> A lot of the time, stories end up in the paper not necessarily because they satisfy any of those categories [of newsworthiness], but because it happened to be moderately interesting, there happened to be a press release about it, and there happened to be a need for a story—a lighter feature, maybe, to balance out heavier stuff in the Sunday paper.

Johnson's description clearly conveys notions of product image imbedded with notions of audience preferences. It assumes that audience members want a particular balance between heavy and light material in the newspaper. However, Johnson's description also supports Fishman's (1982) notion of practical accomplishment:

> The practical accomplishment perspective says that journalists' routine methods for producing news—that is, the very process of "newsgathering"—constructs an image of reality. ... News stories, if they

reflect anything, reflect the practices of the workers in the organizations that produce news. (pp. 219–220)

For Johnson, the stories that the *Tribune* produces are subunits that the organization believes it needs to round out its overall product: the newspaper. Stories are subunits of the newspaper. Good quotes or "sound bites" are subunits of the story. The job of the news organization is to put the pieces together and form a completed product.

Another expression used by journalists to characterize news that is viable is "doable." To be "accomplished," news has to be doable. For WGN asssignment editor Mike Kertez, that means something that will not take more than a day or two to put together:

> I work on a day-to-day basis. The stories that I do have to be done in one day. There are a lot of stories that can't be done in one day; those are not my purview—I don't cover stories like that. ... After years of experience, you know what stories are impossible to do that day. By doing it in a day, that means you have to start and finish it in a day or [2].

A story idea may meet all the other criteria for inclusion in a newscast, but if it cannot be completed that day, it will not be produced, that is, practically accomplished. That same kind of language is used by *Tribune* reporter Bill Recktenwald:

> In choosing a story, you should obviously look at the ability you're going to have to complete the story and how many people does it impact and how good of a story can you come up with and how important is it. ... It's more doable to find out who is defrauding somebody in some kind of scheme, taking money from elderly people, than to spend the rest of your life working on the Kennedy assassination. ... It doesn't do any good if it's sitting on your desk; you have all these notes and you can't put it into the paper. Where it does good is the front page of *The Chicago Tribune* paper.

The most superior product idea does the consumer no good if it can never be accomplished by the news organization.

The notion that news is a practical accomplishment of news workers within organizational structures is also highlighted by discussions about planning. At times, news organizations clearly ready themselves for their "production" task. Hough's text, *News Writing* (1995) made the case that "the production of the newspaper is a series of carefully planned steps beginning with the reporting and writing of a news story and ending with the delivery of the newspaper to a reader's doorstep or a newsstand" (p. 32).

The news is planned in advance and produced by both print and broadcast news organizations when they deem it appropriate. Yoakam and Cremer (1989), for example, applied a football analogy to planning live coverage in broadcast news—the "game plan." They argued that it is important that each news worker know his or her clear assignment. Ironically, WGN employees point to a football story to illustrate how successful preparation paid off in their reporting: the firing of the Chicago Bears' head coach, Mike Ditka. Executive Producer Tony Noce cites planning as the factor that made his product turn out so well:

> We had a day and a half of learning that this was going to happen. ... And it was the preplanning of that kind of story, the getting together with the producer, the news producer, the sports producer, and the sports anchor [that made the reporting effort successful]. All of us got together that night before and over the phone mapped out our plan of attack, how we were going to cover the story.

The key discussion focuses on readying the journalists to carry out their activities. The notion that news coverage can be planned ahead of time is reinforced by *Tribune* political editor Kerry Luft's depiction of his paper's coverage of the fall 1992 elections:

> What made that good was prior planning. We knew, basically, when ... we were planning to do [each story]. When you cover an election, there are stories you can plan to do like Carol Mosely Braun's position on the death penalty, for instance, [and] the profile of the 54th state senate district. You know you're going to do those; you know those are important to do. We had those planned and assigned as much as 3 months in advance. ... That made it very clear what people's responsibilities were going to be and that's why I think we were able to cover pretty much every interesting race in the metropolitan area.

Both the coverage of Ditka's firing and the coverage of the 1992 fall elections illustrate how news coverage can be planned in advance with different tasks assigned to different employees, which supports the notion of news as the result of practical accomplishment. The idea that a great deal of news coverage is planned ahead of time is nothing new for those who work for news organizations. Any credible news organization has a bountiful "futures file" by which the news day is organized, listing meetings, press events, and so forth, that might be covered. Still, for those who fancy the illusion that news is simply a reflection of reality as it spontaneously happens, the image of planned news coverage can be disturbing. Both Chicago newsgathering examples also suggest that producing the news is a group effort. Everyone pitches in to create the news product. In another incident, *Tribune* photo assignment editor Frank Hames characterized his paper's coverage of a mass murder at a fast-food restaurant in Palatine, Illinois, in a way that highlights the coordination of newsworkers and their jobs:

> We had enough people for a Saturday–Sunday paper, and we were able to call in some other people on their days off. … We had four or five photographers that spent 12 to 14 hours standing out in the cold . … It was really just a good team effort. … And when I saw Sunday's paper the next morning, … I thought it really looked good.

The completed news product had come off the assembly line looking polished. News can be planned in advance just as other companies prepare to produce their wares. In addition, each news employee can contribute his or her part in accomplishing the news.

A practical accomplishment perspective suggests that a journalist's routine constructs an image of reality. That routine principally focuses on product image, the creation of news products—stories, newscasts, newspapers. It is within those products that tacit images of the audience are imbedded.

ILLUSTRATIONS OF AN EMPHASIS ON PRODUCT IMAGE

Although journalists may be vague in their discussions of audience, they are clear in talking about news stories and how to produce them. For example, award-winning TV journalist Byron Harris wrote in Biagi's (1987) *NewsTalk II:*

> After you do this work a while, you see a picture and you think, "There's my lead sentence." And, of course, a picture isn't a sentence, but a picture combined with a certain sentence is going to have an effect. So, every time you're out on a story, you think, "That is it. That is the

essence of what I want to say." I see pictures all the time that are sentences, and I have my photographer shoot them. (p. 114)

Newspaper reporters, too, have specific ideas about what components add up to make a good story. For example, *Tribune* reporter Steve Johnson offered some criteria by which he judged a story on the proliferation of handguns in Chicago as good:

> It was a very long story. It had the kind of detail that a lot of newspaper stories don't, mostly because of time constraints, and I had the time to work on it that I needed to put that together. I thought it read well despite its length, and I thought it was pretty easy for readers to get through and told them something, not that they didn't know, but that they may have known, but didn't quite know why they knew it.

For Johnson, then, a good news story has detail, reads well, and offers new information. For *Tribune* reporter George Papajohn, a nicely produced story has detail, depth, and texture:

> Last week the story we did about the gang war and how it affects people at the Robert Taylor homes — that went real well. What I think made it good [was] it had detail, it wasn't just your typical story that says "people got shot, how many people got shot, this is what the police said." It talked about the way the community works, how it's affected, and sort of the ripple effect of what happens when gang violence increases. ... So it sort of had a certain depth and texture that you don't always get from your basic police reporting. It kind of went beyond what we do most of the time.

For Papajohn, a print journalist, a good news product examines the news event within a social context. WGN journalists also have product images. Broadcast journalists know what makes for a usable, successful story—a product that is inherently of quality. For them, quality typically focuses around elements like good visuals, live action, and short, pithy sound bites.

A good deal of discussion also focuses on the tools of production—the equipment. A preoccupation with that equipment reflects news as practical accomplishment and demonstrates journalists' focus on product image. This is especially true for television news. The language used by engineers, producers, and reporters is very often focused on technical proficiency. For example, this was the discussion between a reporter and a photographer on the way out to cover a feature story:

Photographer: I shot this Batman thing this morning. This guy dressed up in a Batman suit climbed up the broken part of the Michigan Avenue bridge.

Reporter: Again? ... It's kind of an annual event. We usually blow it though. Did you get it?

Photographer: Oh yeah. I was right—

Reporter: Don't tell me you shot it handheld.

Photographer: No, I shot it with a tripod.

Reporter: Congratulations. You're the first shooter to ever go down and shoot that with a tripod. Normally, we go down and we get the guy and he is 200 feet in the air — and I don't even want to put it on the air it's so bad.

There is no discussion of whether this is a good piece to air on the news or whether it communicates anything to the audience. There is only discussion of the technical requirements of the shoot. It is not uncommon for television news workers to judge the quality of their work based almost exclusively on organizational and technological considerations. For example, when the noon news producer at WGN is asked what his biggest personal goal is in producing the news, he replies:

At 12:59, to feel good and say, "Hey, that was a good one." There are so many elements that go into a newscast, and you feel like, we had a good mix, we had good remotes, we had good tape packages. You can't pinpoint it on one thing; there are so many elements. I think those of us in newsrooms, there is some kind of a sense, inner feeling, that you come out of a newscast and you know that was a good one. Everybody did their job; nobody slacked off; everybody was in there pitching.

That is likely to be a common response for a producer of a television news show. Yet, it demonstrates a fixation with the technical quality of the news in contrast with a focus on communicating with the audience. The group effort implied also suggests a focus on the process of the news organization. Yet, although all of his talk focuses on product image, his language suggests an implicit knowledge that is not so easy to characterize: "There is some kind of a sense, inner feeling, that you come out of a newscast and you know that was a good one." That inner feeling may have something to do with a tacit knowledge of the audience. He continues:

You get that feeling. I'm a strong believer in just instinct, rather than those Q-ratings, where they take people and they wire them and they probe them with this, that, and the other thing just to see how they react to anchors and things like that.

That is, the producer uses his instincts to gauge audience reaction to the news.

A focus on practical accomplishment by the news organization and attention to product image is perhaps best illustrated in the unfolding of a television spot-news story that allows for the station to use a "live shot" from the scene for its noon newscast. The staff in the newsroom first becomes cognizant of a shooting at an area high school at about 10:30 a.m., 1½ hours prior to the noon news. Assignment manager Bernie Colleran updates the station's executive producer, Tony Noce, and assistant news director Jim Disch about the morning's stories:

Colleran: Tilton [High School] originally said nobody was seriously injured. There was a shooting but no was seriously hurt.

Noce: It was in the school, though. Whenever it's in the school, that makes it more [newsworthy] than if they're shot outside the school.

Disch: Particularly if it's a gun and whether they have metal detectors.

Noce: Why don't we send [anchor/reporter Robert] Jordan on his way to the schools?

Colleran: Because then you end up with Muriel [another noontime reporter] with no crews and Jordan's package [a feature story Jordan has not finished producing] disappearing. ... One of these two stories is not going to be worth a package.

Disch: I'm just guessing that Tilton's going to not end up being much. ... For live, [a live story for the noon news] you've got Muriel anyway, right?

Noce: The thing I'm afraid of, not sending anyone to Tilton, is [missing] the principal and all that going over the story about the gun detectors not being [turned on] ... The "high-tech school" [Jordan's unfinished feature] — we've got interview, we've got B-roll, you can have anybody wrap it [put the story together and announce it].

Disch: Actually, Jordan can go down there [to the Tilton High School shooting site] just to cover our ass on the interviews. ... We've got Roseann coming in and everybody comes in ...

Shortly thereafter, the station staff learns from listening to an all-news radio station that one of the youths shot at the school is in serious condition. The decision is made to send anchor/reporter Robert Jordan to report the story.

There is insight in this situation into the workings of the modern TV newsroom. The start of the conversation focuses on elements of newsworthiness. The group focuses on what stories to cover. The initial assumption is that the Tilton school story is a big story because it entails conflict and drama. It also would allow for live coverage during the noon newscast—something the station sees as a big asset. There is a shooting inside the school. This is a school already equipped with metal detectors that should have detected a gun. Obviously, something failed. (Underlying assumptions regarding the criteria of newsworthiness are considered in chapters 3 and 4.)

The assignment editor focuses on the practicality of getting the stories aired for the noon newscast. He argues that if Jordan is sent out to cover the story, that would leave another reporter without a camera crew and another story that Jordan had planned to finish not getting completed for the noon newscast. The way the news is covered and the stories that are selected for more detailed coverage say something about the focus of the news operation and its technical capabilities. For WGN, that means a maximum of two live shots at noon (there are two trucks equipped for live coverage). In addition, a live story is considered a necessity because these news workers believe a live story adds something to the newscast for the viewer.

In spot news, there is some confusion about just what is really happening. Thus far, the station has relied on reports that an all-news radio station has aired. Noce has expressed concern about not sending anyone to Tilton High School, the site of the shooting. The station runs a noon newscast but doesn't have another until 9:00 p.m. That gives it a chance to get a jump on the other television stations in town that do not air a noon newscast. Disch opts to send out a live unit to the school. Within 15 minutes, Jordan and a "live truck" are on their way to the high school.

An emphasis on product image is reflected in Jordan's dialogue with his news team back at the station. He communicates from the car heading to the scene by cellular telephone. His side of the conversation sounds like this:

> Is there tape? I take it Mabel is shooting now. … If necessary, I can feed live if we're getting close. I'll just hot-feed it to you if I get a byte. I'll try to grab somebody and we'll do something. We'll get it on, don't worry about it. And I'm first? You want a stand-up; you want a scene-setter. I need some information. We've got three people shot. Do you know their conditions? … We're going to have to send that tape in.

The live crew is behind me. So we're going to [carry] the tape back in? ... I don't think he's going to make it though [back to the station for the airing of the noon newscast]. We're going to get [to the scene] at about 11:15 or 11:20. ... He gets back with the tape, if he's fast, about 12. We'll be cutting it real close. ... I'll ask Mabel what she has and I may roll to ... See, we're not going to have any time to cut anything. That's the problem. We're not going to have time to edit anything. ... Okay, I'll give you a call from the scene.

Notice the language used by Jordan in his conversations with the station. He has two principle concerns: the technical requirements of the shoot and any details others may have about the condition of the students who were shot. All of the news workers know what is needed to produce the news product: what information, what types of pictures and interviews are needed, what kind of time the reporter will need to tell the story, and so forth. The sole focus is on producing and airing the story and coordinating with the station, the live truck, and the photographer already on site. Getting the story aired live becomes an intense game of "beat-the-clock."

Once he arrives at the scene, Jordan discovers that all of the other television news stations in town are already at the site. Channel 2, the sensationalistic CBS-owned station, is at the location and is ready to break into programming. Channel 7, the ABC-owned station, has an 11:30 news program and will air a breaking story from the site as well. Another WGN photographer arrives to assist. Jordan learns from a news competitor that one student is dead and the suspects have been taken away in handcuffs. This is clearly a strong enough element to make the live shot at the high school the lead story on the noon newscast, meaning Jordan has less than 40 minutes to prepare his live report.

Jordan uses the time to coordinate with the station and to uncover as much information as possible. He also attempts to get interviews set up for his live story. In the last few minutes before going on the air, Jordan still scrambles to line up interviews. There is a pack of reporters gathered around the high school door as Jordan finalizes his negotiations with the station:

Jordan: Can you hear me? Can you hear me okay? Are they seeing a picture? Bill, can you hear me?

Jordan calls out to a police detective who is ready to issue a statement to the crowd: "We're live here. Come over here." When the detective doesn't move to Jordan, Jordan moves in as close to the detective as possible to begin his story:

Police Detective: We had three people shot in the school; we have one fatal. We have one fatal male [who] was shot in the chest; we have one shot in the rib and one shot in the toe. We have one person in custody who is in the hospital who got hit by a car at 47th and Union, trying to evade police. We're in the process ...

Jordan backs away from the mob of reporters gathered outside the school and continues his report:

Jordan: Right now, we are in the midst of a press conference here being given by Detective ...

Jordan's story goes on to focus on the knowledge he has garnered up to this point. After the report is finished, he spends another 40 minutes polishing his information for a second report toward the end of the hour-long newscast. After the stories were completed, Jordan offered this assessment of his goals for the stories:

The first thing that's going through my mind is structure—how am I going to structure the live shot? How much information do I have? Is it accurate? And what can I go with and what should I not go with? What kind of tape do I have? How am I going to get the tape back? How much time do I have? Can I pull a sound byte? Will I have to do like we did the second time, pull a byte from the truck and feed it back? That saves them the time of having to try to run through the tape. Because I know what I've got. And generally, that's about it. If I know all the elements that I have, then I can pretty well go ahead and structure the piece. You know I can grab some people, go with it, and put it together.

The reporter's description shows the priorities in spot news reporting and, seemingly, in most of his work: putting together the news product to make it as smooth as possible without making any factual mistakes. Observing the news process reveals that both print and broadcast reports are clearly "produced." They are the product of the routines and technologies available to the news organization. Yet, although there is no explicit discussion of the audience in the planning of the piece, expectations about audience are certainly built into the process. Jordan contends that his station's use of live coverage of an event builds in notions of immediacy for his audience:

They [the audience] have come to learn that if they get it from me or if they get it [information] from the police, it's supposed to be accurate. ... So, if I let them get it immediately from the police, that information flow is not going secondhand. It has that immediacy. ... It's like you are hearing it live, as it's happening, from the horse's mouth.

Perceptions of the audience feed product image. Jordan's understandings about audience acceptance of information led him to begin his story with a live statement from the police detective. Although he is mostly cognizant of his product (story) as he works on it, notions of audience interest are built into the news formulae.

ILLUSTRATIONS OF THE TACIT AUDIENCE

The notion that news is simply a manufactured product sells the process short. Even though there is often a fixation with the technical requirements of producing the news, there are tacit understandings of the audience that support what journalists do. For example, Schudson (1995) argued that within news interviewing, five parties may be implicitly involved: the reporter, the source, the reporter's employing institution, the source's institution, and what he called the *absent audience*. Indeed, images of the audience help shape the entire newsgathering process. For example, demographic understandings about the audience can help shape the form of the WGN noon newscast, according to writer/producer Tim Jackson:

We have a high percentage of the audience that are middle-aged or above. So, therefore, we pay particular attention, especially in the midday news, to stories that affect people, [age] 55 plus. .... An example of that might be if there's a dramatic change in health care costs. We really focus on that and will zoom on in our preparation to say, "What does that really mean to somebody?"

Although that demographic information doesn't dictate content at the station, it does give the news workers an image by which they can interpret the news and coordinate the selection of news stories. Similarly, audience concerns are real and do fit into the process of selecting front-page news at *The Chicago Tribune*, according to metro editor Jean Davidson:

It's a gut decision. It's something that we make on an individual case every day. And it's almost thoughtless after a period of time. And I can tell you, quickly, by reading down my schedule that there may be three candidates I'd consider today and the rest I wouldn't at all. It gets down to, I guess, how many people are affected, whether it's a catastrophe, whether there's an element of it that is particularly interesting or new or unusual—quirky—if it is a broad trend story or a ground-breaking story. All of those things are part of this very quick process.

Davidson's language suggests that audience concerns are an implicit part of the understanding by which front-page stories are selected. Those concerns are typically imbedded in notions of what makes one story more newsworthy than another. Audience concerns are talked about in terms of "interest," or in terms of "how many people are effected," and so forth. Yet, she described the front-page selection process as "almost thoughtless," a knowledge system akin to what Schön described as knowing-in-action. Schön (1983) wrote, "There are actions, recognitions, and judgments which we know how to carry out spontaneously; we do not have to think about them prior to or during their performance" (p. 54).

Much of the journalists' understandings of their audiences are internalized in this way. Both the technical requirements of producing the news and the news values that characterize the news are imbued with a sense of the audience. Yet, much of that knowledge is buried within the journalists' everyday functioning. The company that produces baseball bats does not think explicitly about the user each time it manufactures a bat; it has considered how the prospective user will hold the bat when it designs the product. So, when manufacturing the bat, the company whittles down its handle for the person who will someday swing it. Similarly, the audience isn't brought to immediate cognizance each time the journalist works. As one WGN reporter said, "Here our mission is just simply to get it on the air most of the time." Still, the audience is a very real consideration in the overall news construction process. The audience has been considered in the tacit assumptions built into the job tasks, the news format, and technologies. For example, when assignment manager Bernie Colleran talks about television equipment, he does not explicitly talk about the audience:

> The cost to buy one [uplink truck] is about $300,000, $350,000, or something like that. ... So it was a very expensive proposition. ... More and more we're expected to produce live for sports—very much for sports—and news.

Clearly, there is a fascination with the equipment in television news production. Yet, Colleran implies that fascination grows out of internal expectations within the station stemming from its expectations about what the public demands:

> Ourselves, based on the public's expectations and competition. If two other stations in town are live and you ain't, your news director gets a little call from the station manager saying, "Why ain't we live?" "Well, you're expecting us to save money." He says, "Not that much. I get embarrassed when we ain't live."

Note how Colleran's description matches Ryan and Peterson's (1982) assertions about product image: "Having a product image is to shape a piece of work so that it is most likely to be accepted by decision makers at the next link in the chain" (p. 25). The assignment editor seeks to please the news director while the reporters seek to please their editors. Implicit in this assignment editor's notion that the station needs to spend money for its news is also the expectation that the audience demands that type of coverage. It is also imbedded in the notion that the station must compete with its television rivals. If the station does not serve up a technically sophisticated news product, it will lose face with both its audience and the competition. If the competition is serving up live coverage and your station is not, there is the implicit fear that audience members will slip away.

Audience considerations are built into the newsmaking process in a variety of ways. For example, at Tribune broadcasting, WGN, and the company's other stations periodically exchange news, each station using each other's call letters at the end. This is designed to give the audience members the impression that the local station has reporters "on the road." Occasionally, WGN reporters will take on the persona of the viewer in their reporting as they speak with sources. For example, one reporter queried his source, "Do you know what most of our viewers are thinking at this very moment?" WGN assistant news director Jim Disch says that style of questioning is encouraged:

> You're trying to make the story meaningful to your viewer, so if you're talking to the economics professor, sooner or later, you're going to have to say in very polite terms, "Let's cut out the college lecture. Tell my white-collar and blue-collar audience out there in very basic terms how this will effect them." And you're really telling them, give me a meaningful statement for our viewers and [in] a lot of cases, you have to speak in terms of that because of the time limitations. ("That was a great 2-minute answer. Can you try it again for my viewer in 30 seconds?")

Varying graphic presentations of the news are also clearly de-signed to assist the television viewer and the newspaper reader. For example, when WGN presents more than one report on the same topic, Disch says graphics are used to assist the viewer:

"Team coverage tonight begins with" ... Even if you don't call it team coverage, when you're starting into the sequence, do a full-page graphic or something and then do the very quick bullet points of what we're going to be covering during the next few minutes—point one, point two, and point three in terms of where your reporters are—and then go into the sequence. So, now you're kind of setting the table for the viewers. ... And I think it just reinforces to the viewer that you really are doing a lot of coverage.

Again, news producers may not explicitly think about the audi-ence each time they decide to use bullet points, but at some point, the decision to use bullet points was predicated on an understanding of how the audience views the news. Eventually that decision be-comes internalized, and an explicit understanding of the audience is not consciously considered, just as Schön (1983) maintained:

There are actions, recognitions, and judgments which we know how to carry out spontaneously; we do not have to think about them prior to or during their performance. ... In some cases, we were once aware of the understandings that were subsequently internalized in our feeling for the stuff of action. (p. 54)

Those who design newspaper presentation also consider the audi-ence, and the audience seems to care. *Tribune* managing editor Dick Ciccone spoke about seemingly small changes made at his paper:

You change the sports television calendar as we did a couple of weeks ago—we put some new logos and darkened the halftone, made it difficult to read—you have 10 to 12 people call you up the first morning you do that. "What the hell did you do to the sports calendar?" Ten to 12 people is an awful lot of people to call this newspaper. I mean, you go and look at it. In this case, it was so clear that we had really screwed it up. ... So, what the hell did we do? Change it back. ... So, do we respond to readers? Sure.

In reaction to those phone calls, the newspaper tailored its product to those very specific audience demands. Tacit notions of the audience are also a part of the overall philosophical approach taken at the paper. Ciccone says about the front page:

> I think the philosophy I try to achieve every day is that on the front page, you create a mix of national, international, and foreign news that has the potential to have the greatest impact on how people conduct their lives. In that mix, whenever possible, you try and create islands of entertainment. ... You don't need to know that to get through the day, but it's part of our culture, our history. Certainly if you can write a story about stress that is kind of easy and enjoyable to read with your cup of coffee—that's part of the goal.

This informal understanding of audience is another example of knowing-in-action. What were once, perhaps, cognizant understandings of the audience become imbedded in the everyday activities of the news organization. Sometimes the audience understandings were never consciously employed in the news construction process. Still, they were subconsciously recognized as important and built into the news product.

The tacit audience in the news construction process is illustrated in the following exchange between a *Tribune* reporter and the acting metro editor as they discussed an assignment that the reporter had just completed. They were trying to determine whether the event merited a feature story in the paper. The reporter had spent an hour and a half at an exhibit in a Chicago hotel on "The Classroom of the Future" sponsored by several business firms. The two news workers' conversation went like this:

> **Editor**: I mean, was there anything inherently interesting at the scene of the kids hooking up with ...?
> **Reporter**: Not particularly. They all had their little Ameritech T-shirts on ... and it was basically kind of a bore, to tell you the truth. Kind of a boring lesson too that she was teaching.
> **Editor**: Okay. Well, I guess we'll pull the plug on it then. I mean it doesn't sound like it was a story at all.
> **Reporter**: Nancy took some pictures. Yeah, the only way I could see it was a story if one of these schools was really considering using a big chunk of their Title I funding.

Not once during the exchange between reporter and editor is the audience explicitly mentioned. Still, a tacit audience is built into this process in the notions of newsworthiness that the two discuss. For example, the editor's first question pertains to a news value closely linked to audience concern: interest. The implicit question is, "Would the reader find anything interesting in this story?" The editor takes on the persona of audience advocate. "Is there anything that happens within this event that would benefit our audience?" The reporter initially answers no. There is nothing interesting. Soon, however, she qualifies her answer, couched in another news value: impact. If the school is using Title I funding, the public is footing the bill out of money designated for disadvantaged youth. The audience is implicitly entitled to know how it is spending its money. A bit later the conversation continues:

> **Editor**: So, essentially all it was was a screen up there and they were just able to see into the classroom.
> **Reporter**: In the set-up there is a display with little booths. But one thing that was neat was they had a disabled man who was with a voice-operated computer technology. So, I mean, all of this stuff applies not just to education but to, as they were pointing out, the health care field and this and that and the other thing. It seems like their bottom line was we need to get this stuff more readily available to everyone. Nancy was taking pictures of … and then their P.R. flacks were practically clinging on my shoulders the whole time I walked around.
> **Editor**: It doesn't sound like much. In the meantime, my other reservation is that we just found out that a brand new Chicago public school opened today and no one seemed to know about it. I mean it's a new middle school and I think we're going to do a feature on that. I'm thinking how this could be one too many Chicago public school [stories]—plus there's another Chicago public school story developing.—Well, is this being used anywhere or is this just purely a demonstration?
> **Reporter**: Right now the point is it's too expensive. Like $30,000 to $50,000 dollars, so I think he said that, "No, it's not being used."—So, it's not used here yet. So mainly it was teachers going "Yes, I'd love to have this."

The reporter sees further impact for her audience in terms of the wide application of the technology into other fields. Acting as "audience advocate" herself, she finds interest in the disabled man using voice-operated computer technology. But, bottom line, the technology does not yet have real impact for the school districts and the audience because it is still too expensive to be feasible.

The *Tribune* editor is concerned with overall product image. She voices concern that this could be one too many Chicago public school stories. Her viewpoint is wider than the reporter who is strictly concerned with her story. The editor is concerned with the whole newspaper product. She believes it requires a sense of balance. (Contrasting organizational viewpoints pertaining to audience are treated in chapter 5). The exchange between editor and reporter concludes:

> **Editor**: Well, this sounds a little bit overly commercial to me. I thought, you know, it was one of these things that, it sounded like it could be something, or it could be nothing and, I mean, what's your gut feeling? I mean, if you had to write the story, is there a way to write it that ...?
>
> **Reporter**: See, my feeling is that not unless I could talk to people that were really opposed to this sort of technology in schools and obviously no one [was] there. There was only one view proposed, and everyone I talked to obviously is like "Oh, this is great." So, unless I could talk to people who really don't think this is a good trend in education, then there's really nothing that makes it a story.

Both reporter and editor are concerned about the strong link to one business. The editor labels the story "overly commercial" and the reporter refers to "P. R. flacks." In addition, the reporter is concerned that only one point of view is presented—that of those in support of the high technology. The reporter believes that to present a "fair" story to her audience, both sides need to be presented. The reporter is concerned with a sense of balance in her story just as the editor is concerned with a sense of balance in the paper as a whole. She too, is concerned with product image—constructing a news story that is fair and objective. By limiting the scope of her story, the reporter acts as sort of a "knowledge arbiter" for her audience, protecting them from sources that are overly zealous in presenting their viewpoint. This logic is common in many journalism texts. For example, Herbert Strentz (1978) wrote:

> If a reporter is to maintain a sense of perspective and some usefulness to employer and audience, he or she must recognize that news sources who might mislead the reporter do not always do so deliberately.—To paraphrase Lippman, we most often see what we want to see or hear what we want to hear. (p. 14)

Toward the end of their conversation, the editor asks the reporter to make a decision about the story based on her "gut feeling." The question again suggests Schön's concept of knowing-in-action. The reporter makes an assessment of the story based on some rational argument but also on internalized, tacit knowledge of her business and of the audience for whom she writes.

The story idea was killed, but the exchange between reporter and editor offers insight into the practical accomplishment of news construction, product image, and the tacit audience imbedded in the process.

CONCLUSION

Although the central concern of journalists is creating the news, tacit understandings of the audience are imbedded in the news gathering process, in the news values they use, and in the technology they use. In the case of the spot-news report, the broadcast journalist and his organization's emphasis on live news reporting is supported by implicit assumptions that audience members deem live reporting more important, timely, and credible than other forms of reporting. Whether those assumptions are accurate or not, they do contribute to the way the stories are presented. Such assumptions lead to even more use of live technologies that reinforce the assumptions. The assumptions are developed in the reporting process—the "knowing" is in the "doing." In the newspaper feature, implicit understandings of the audience accentuate professional values of interest, impact, and objectivity. These values, in turn, help shape the news product—in this case, by killing the feature.

Images of the audience are not easily detected because the audience is not explicitly addressed very often. Yet, it is a mistake to therefore assume that the audience is not an important component of the news construction process. Understandings about the audience are built into news values in much the way implicit news values are built into the news process. For example, as illustrated, timeliness becomes a key consideration in the broadcast news formula, often taking precedence over depth of analysis. Implicit in that elevation of the news value of timeliness is an understanding that the audience turns to TV or the radio for the latest details, not for substantive interpretative reporting. There is little, if any, discussion by the news workers during the breaking news story about that understanding; however, that understanding girds what they do. In chapters 3 and 4, I argue that key news values are imbedded with tacit notions of the audience as I examine each of several news values.

Chapter 3

The Tacit Audience in News Values: Timeliness, Proximity, Conflict, and Prominence

Although news values say a great deal about what constitutes news, they are also imbedded with assumptions about the news audience. The way the news values are interpreted and used can tell us a great deal about how news workers and news organizations perceive their audiences.

Textbook definitions of news typically hinge on factors or values of newsworthiness. A fairly representative list of news factors is provided in Itule and Anderson's (1987) reporting text, *News Writing and Reporting for Today's Media*. Their list of six factors includes: timeliness, proximity, conflict, eminence (or prominence), consequence (or impact), and human interest. In this book I argue that each of these news values is supported by tacit understandings of the audience. In this chapter, I explore the way perceptions of audience shape and support the first four factors: timeliness, proximity, conflict, and prominence. In the next chapter I examine the final two factors: impact and interest.

Although experienced journalists are more reticent to explicitly cite these news values and are more apt to cite "gut instinct" as the determinant of newsworthiness, much of their discussion typically comes back to a reliable cadre of news factors. Therefore, in some sense for journalists, news values represent defining attributes of the "news event."

Yet, it has also been argued that news values reflect the work process in which the journalist is employed. As journalists engage in efforts to construct stories day after day, they employ a set of criteria that enables them to more efficiently construct those stories. Journalists know which criteria will assist them in most efficiently constructing those stories to meet various demands: deadlines, peer acceptance, favorable treatment by the editors, and so forth. Therefore, rather than simply identifying an event as newsworthy, news values also function to help routinize the news process for journalists. Berkowitz (1992) wrote, "Routinizing newswork makes outcomes more predictable, increasing the chances that newsworkers will meet their organizational expectations. It takes amorphous public occurrences and turns them into discrete manageable chunks" (p. 82). For instance, by arguing that certain events are the most timely, and therefore the most important stories, the news factor of timeliness seems to dictate that live shots are an essential component of the broadcast news show.

Just as news values help define and shape the news, they also carry forth assumptions about the audience, and those assumptions further shape the news. For instance, to argue that news must be timely suggests that the news audience has a strong appetite for knowing the latest details in a breaking story and quickly tires of "old" news. It suggests a particular sort of active audience, more concerned with recency than with depth and understanding. In arguing that news must have proximity, one implies that the audience is more parochial, concerned with personally relevant news, than cosmopolitan, concerned more with world affairs and global trends.

Evolving perceptions of the audience that stem from daily news gathering activities can elevate or diminish these news values and can help shape their meaning. Typically, journalists form perceptions of the audience as they engage in the news process and as they rely on standard story types. For example, as journalists regularly produce stories to beat deadlines, they come to understand the audience as one concerned with the latest breaking news. Similarly, as journalists repeatedly produce the standard story on a house fire, they come to understand the audience as mesmerized by poignant pictures and by illustrations of human drama and conflict.

The following discussion illustrates the ways in which perceptions of the audience are embedded in the news process and within the key news values that help define that work.

TIMELINESS

By definition, news is timely. Past events or trends no longer qualify as news. That is true for both broadcast and print entities. Yet, when considered from the viewpoint of the modern audience member, print journalists and broadcast journalists part ways dramatically. To the modern broadcast journalist, timeliness increasingly translates into not just recency, but rather, immediacy. For print journalists who come to realize that they cannot compete with their broadcast peers in offering their audience the most timely news, the emphasis on the news value can be seen as their opportunity to offer the audience a distinct alternative to broadcast news. Rather than seeing their broadcast counterparts as competitors, they sometimes view them as allies, whetting an audience's appetite for further coverage on a breaking story.

Traditionally, notions of timeliness have been considered one of the genuine differences between print and broadcast journalism. As Gamson (1984) wrote, "Television journalists believe they have an edge in immediacy over other media. By showing viewers films of events, they make these events nearer and more real" (p. 56). In addition, new electronic news gathering (ENG) technologies have enabled local television newsrooms to focus on more timely and even live reports, according to Yoakam and Cremer (1989): "In television newsrooms across the United States, news personnel are working at a much faster pace sometimes on the ragged edge where editorial control becomes a problem" (p. 3). The technology can sometimes lead to a prominence of form over substance. Mayer (1993) referred to it as a miracle: "The miracle of broadcast is the live event, the accurate if not necessarily truthful simulacrum of something that is happening, as it is happening" (p. 73).

That focus seems borne out at WGN. Writer/producer Tim Jackson suggests that television technology and its perceived use by his audience has heightened the role that immediacy plays in terms of newsworthiness:

> I think [new technology] really changes the focus of how people learn about news and information. It therefore changes the focus of what's important. 'Cause they're now getting information all day long. ... Now they can watch news all day and all night long, almost anywhere they are in the world and ... with either a phone, or television or satellite dish or a pocket computer, they're going to be able to get a lot of information.

Jackson hints that competitive technologies such as all-news cable channels are changing the definition of local news, but so are technologies that are not yet fully realized. Although most viewers likely do not yet own a satellite dish or a pocket computer, he suggests that his station's coverage is starting to proceed as if they did:

> There's a very *now* kind of voice that wasn't around 10 years ago. Well, the chocolate cookie factory that's on fire is happening now and that's why it's important. It may not effect very many people. Whereas when we had the longer view, where you went to work at 8 o'clock in the morning and when you got home at 5:30 or 6, you sort of had the news on while you were taking care of your kids or initiating your evening life—well, now you have a TV in your car or you have it in your office or wherever. So, I think *now,* what's happening *now* has become more important—for better or for worse because that changes the ability of us to put things in perspective.

At WGN, Jackson contends that the news has become more "short-term, very headline-oriented and very dramatic." That is clearly evident in the station's fascination with airing live reports during almost every newscast. Reporter/anchor Robert Jordan explains the attraction of doing live coverage, "Live ... gives more immediacy to the situation and ... in the hierarchy of importance, I guess you might say people tend to believe that because you're live, the story takes on a greater importance."

The news value of timeliness seems to have been replaced by the value of immediacy, thanks to television technology. Yet, what seems to be news construction that is entirely driven by technological capability is predicated on assumptions about the audience and what will interest them. Implicit perceptions of the audience are described by the journalist in explaining the station's frequent use of live reports:

> It lets the viewer[s] know that they're getting the latest information rather than something that was taped and sent back. ... The information flow at first is erratic and sometimes not accurate but at least ... you have a live source saying it. ... So, not only is it firsthand and it's immediate, but it also has more of a symbolic importance because it's coming from an authority figure.

Thus, Jordan sees the immediacy of the live reporting as adding credibility to his newscast. The tacit notions of the audience are invoked in justifying and explaining not only the story's timeliness, but also its form: erratic and sometimes not accurate, but from live sources.

WGN assignment manager Bernie Colleran argues, however, that competition is a keen concern in the striving for live reports—perhaps as important as is the perceived audience. He says his news team is expected more and more to produce live news and sports reports: "Actually, it's more peer expectation. It's not really a public expectation, although, it's a perceived public expectation, ratings-wise ... it's purely perceived, as opposed to gauged." Thus, peers also form an important audience in helping shape the construction of the news. In this case, the peers lead to an emphasis on live reporting. That professional culture which highlights immediacy often invokes public expectations to justify the fixation on live reporting.

Although the imperative to produce live reports may be justified by notions of the audience (or of the competition), they may not actually be serving audience needs. Schudson (1986), for example, argued:

> The pressure journalists are under to be first is generated internally in news organizations. No one in the audience gives a damn if ABC beats CBS by two seconds or not. The journalist's interest in immediacy hangs on as an anachronistic ritual of the media tribe. Getting the story first is a matter of journalistic pride, but one that has little to do with journalistic quality or public service. (pp. 80–81)

Although Schudson may be right that no one in the audience cares if ABC beats CBS by 2 seconds, it may be too simplistic to argue that notions of immediacy are simply a matter of "journalistic pride." News workers at WGN clearly voice a rationale for live shots. Executive producer Tony Noce sees the live story as qualitatively better for his audience:

> I think it's an initial gut feeling that if you're there live, you can make the story more immediate and tell it better. When you first make that decision and say "yes, let's go out there and do it live," you might not think or have it totally laid out in your thought process that it's going to be better being live, but whatever it takes to be there live, you have to take that chance and say, "yes, this is a live kind of story" and sometimes you're right and sometimes you're wrong.

Much of news discussion focuses around talk like "gut feelings." This sense of covering the news and learning the trade by instinct illustrates Schön's notion of knowing-in-action:

It does not stretch common sense very much to say that the know-how is in the action—that a tight-rope walker's know-how, for example lies in, and is revealed by, the way he takes his trip across the wire, or that a big-league pitcher's know-how is in his way of pitching to a batter's weakness. (p. 51)

It also does not stretch common sense very much to say that a journalist's knowledge of a story that will work for his audience is in his "gut feeling that if you're there live, you can make the story more immediate and tell it better." The journalist cannot clearly describe what it is about going live that makes the report so much better for his audience, and yet his gut feelings tell him that live reporting is superior. That gut feeling often stems, too, from an understanding of the journalist's peers and competition. Serving the audience and beating the competition become intertwined into a gut feeling concerning timeliness and immediacy. It becomes the tacit understanding about how to do a story—the knowing-in-action.

For other news stories, the fascination with timeliness at the station appears to focus on having the best visuals, which are only thought to be available as a story happens. If the news event is more than a couple of hours old, the news is often thought to be cold or stale. For example, reporter Mary Gannon told her photographer why she argued so vehemently with the assignment desk over not covering a traffic accident that left three people dead in a Chicago suburb at 11:00 one morning (this dialogue occurred later that afternoon):

> **Gannon**: He wanted us to go to Orland Park for three dead in a traffic accident. He's nuts. I mean it happened at 11 o'clock this morning. What do you think we're going to get now? By the time that we get there it's going to be dark.
> **Photographer**: Three dead. We should cover it instead of the stringers.
> **Gannon**: Well, you want to go there?
> **Photographer**: No.
> **Gannon**: By the time we get there, there isn't going to be anything left to shoot. That's the problem.
> **Photographer**: It would take us at least 45 minutes.

The reporter weighs the notion of covering the accident with the value of what her report could visually show. In this instance, the news is or is not covered depending on the ease with which the videotape can be attained. The reporter asks her photographer, "Well, you want to go there?" He answers, "No." The story is therefore much less likely to be covered. This is another example of news as practical accomplishment. In this instance, the story is considered less newsworthy because the news staff cannot easily get any timely coverage of the event. Without clear visuals, the story is worth less to the station (and presumably to the audience) and is therefore less likely to be covered.

Last, focusing on the most timely stories helps a broadcast show do what newspapers cannot do. The airing of more up-to-date and live stories is believed to be what television is all about. Assistant news director Jim Disch argues that television news needs to demonstrate its strengths to its viewers:

> It gives the viewer a feeling that you are seeing not what you say at the midday show ... but you're seeing the latest stuff that [your staff] can put together. You've got to capitalize on what are the major differences between television and the newspaper.

Newspapers, too, are very cognizant of those differences. At the *Tribune,* there seems to be little concern these days for being "scooped" by the broadcast media. In fact, *Tribune* reporter Steve Johnson contends that the paper can actually benefit by being scooped by broadcast:

> The TV–radio question is one that's always sort of bothered me. It seems to be a theory that if a big story happens at noon on a Tuesday and it's all over TV that night, then we as a newspaper that isn't coming out until the next day, are going to downplay that story a little bit or maybe not give it quite the same prominence that it would have had. And my feeling has always been sort of the opposite.

Johnson argues that while TV will only devote a couple of minutes to a story, the newspaper can provide much more depth and detail. That explanation matches with the wisdom of the paper's managing editor, Dick Ciccone. He says that major news stories aired on TV stimulate further sales of his newspaper. One such story was the outbreak of war in President Bush's Operation Desert Storm:

> It's a war you watch live. You want to watch a Polar-A [sic] missile, travel 600 miles and hit a doorway in Baghdad. Show it to you live—we sell 40,000 more papers the next day. Major events that television covers just stimulate the sale of newspapers because there is an

inherent belief among readers that "I see it live, but I've got to get the real story. Where do I get that? I get it from the newspaper."

The editor, too, voices implicit assumptions about his audience that lead to a different interpretation of timeliness than might have been voiced by the newspaper editor of 40 years ago. That is not to argue that the paper is completely indifferent to notions of timeliness. Reporter Johnson admits that some stories, if overly covered by TV and not as significant as the war in Iraq, may be buried farther back in the paper than if TV had not covered them. Managing editor Ciccone also contends that the advent of CNN has had a marked impact on his paper's coverage:

CNN becomes a competitor over and over.—The day Yeltsin was elected President of the Russian Republic—the first elections they had before the coup ... at 5:00 (p.m.) I ... said, "What do we lead the paper with?" And everybody said "Yeltsin ha[s] been elected president." I said, "You can't—I was shaving at 7 this morning and heard him on CNN thanking the people for his mandate. If I put that headline on my own porch tomorrow morning, I'm going to think I've got yesterday's paper.

Notice that the editor uses himself as representative of his reading audience. An explicit understanding about timeliness develops out of an implicit understanding of his audience, patterned after himself. That matches Gans' (1979) conclusions about the journalists he viewed: "Even when they judged a story by whether it would 'grab' or bore the reader or viewer, and I asked them how they made this judgment, they would generally respond: 'Well, if it bores me, it will bore them'" (pp. 236–237).

In the Yeltsin example, the CNN technology, merged with a sense of how the audience uses the technology, helped Ciccone develop a 1990s version of timeliness for the newspaper. That carries over into coverage. Ciccone continued, "So we had to call up Moscow and have them read and write and say, 'the election of Yeltsin could signal the eventual disintegration of the Soviet Federation.' Now it's a different headline, a little different story."

Notions of audience here are not necessarily embedded in findings from detailed readership studies, but are derived from "doing" the news day in and day out for years. The broadcast journalist makes assumptions about how interested her audience is in a "fatals" story that is several hours old. She comes to an even heightened view of the news value timeliness—because she determines that a shot of a "fatal" hours after the event would be of little interest to her audience. The newspaper editor implicitly learns about his audience after wrestling with his staff over the angle to play up in the Yeltsin story. He identifies with his audience and senses that he would be disappointed with a headline that offered him the same news he had heard the day before on CNN. Some sense of immediacy, or at least "advancing a story" is heightened based on this particular experience of doing the news and thinking about the audience. As journalists construct the news on a daily basis and consider how they or their audience might use the information, they form new impressions of their audience, of their task, and of the values that define news in the first place.

PROXIMITY

Generally, news is considered "immediate." That refers to place, as well as time. The closer to the news audience in time or place, the more the news worker is likely to consider the event "news." Yet, the modern journalist is faced with a not-so-modern predicament, the perception that his or her audience is ultimately concerned with the ultraproximate (what happened in their own families and neighborhoods), rather than just the proximate (nearby). That is particularly difficult in large urban areas such as Chicago. Therefore, journalists look for strategies to tie the outside world to the proximate world of their audience members. Even when technologies enable them to share events happening far away, the strategic goal is to find a way to apply those happenings to the immediate lives of their audience members.

Both news reporters and news sources are aware of those strategies. For example, Morton and Warren (1992) discovered that newspaper editors were more likely to publish press releases that highlighted a local angle than ones that simply originated locally. In his seminal text, *Reporting,* Charnley (1975) tied the immediacy of locale to both audience interest and importance:

> Being close to a news event gives it added interest for the consumer,
> and often added importance. A man can relate more readily to an auto
> smashup, a union picket line, or a campaign speech if he can picture
> its scene, place it among people he knows, or imagine himself as
> spectator or participant. (p. 54)

All things being equal, something is more likely to be considered news if it happens around the corner than if it happens around the world. Tuchman (1978), meanwhile, implied that location is a function of the news gathering process, not just a function of news definition:

> The news net imposes order on the social world because it enables news events to occur at some locations but not at others. Obviously, reporters cannot write about occurrences hidden from view by their social location, that is, either their geographic location or social class. (pp. 23–24)

Kaniss (1991) argued that local media display an urban myopia in their reporting. She attributed this focus on the city (in contrast to the suburbs) to several factors: some professional and some personal. She argued that city agencies are better suited to assist journalists in putting together stories and that journalists see the city as "more important than the suburbs—and more interesting" (p. 76).

Yoakam and Cremer (1989) argued that the advent of ENG technology in local television newsrooms has altered notions of proximity: "They [television newsrooms] also have developed a definition of news that is a much more wide-angle view of the world to be reported on each day" (p. 3). Both Kaniss' and Yoakam and Cremer's contentions can be investigated in light of journalists' and news organizations' views of their audiences.

At times, WGN seemingly works to build a broader image of its geographic scope, congruent with Yoakam and Cremer's "more wide-angle view of the world." For example, one technique used by WGN during the 1992 presidential campaign was that of trading reports with other Tribune-owned stations, all of which ended their reports with varying outcues to give each station the appearance of a national news staff. For example, a station in Atlanta covered the national race in the South and customized one version of the report by closing it with the outcue "WGN News."

The station also shares Washington reporters with other Tribune stations. The station is free to use these stories each day. It can also pay an added fee to get the reporter to put together a special package for the Chicago market. In essence, it gives the impression that WGN has a larger exclusive number of reporters covering a wider geographic scope than it actually does.

Yoakam and Cremer's (1989) assertion that the geographic scope of local TV operations is widening due to changes in technology is also supported by the news generation methods at WGN. Producer/writer Tim Jackson talks about the capabilities:

I think one of the very exciting things about [television news] is the demand and the possibility of being omnipresent. Even though that is a very dangerous concept and often is very misused. ... I can remember 10 or 12 years ago that we were just amazed that we could make microwaves go through the air and get a live shot somewhere from this little truck that looked like it delivered chicken. ... And it's taken us much of the last decade to really take this for granted. Well, now we can do all sorts of things. ... And we're going to be able to do even more.

WGN staffers admit to letting the technology direct the coverage a bit at first. The notion that a local station could air coverage from around the globe was an exciting prospect. Yet now they contend that their field has matured and is using technology less just for technology's sake. Seemingly, it has taken the station some time to understand when the value of the technology to air things from "everywhere" really best serves its audience or when it simply shows off its technology.

Although WGN uses CNN for most of its national and international coverage, it acts fairly independently in town. And the station's news director, Paul Davis, pleads guilty to Kaniss' charge of an urban myopia:

We're all quick to use Chicago stories—Chicago proposing a tax increase—but do people in Shaumburg give a shit? And our audience is significantly not Chicago, so we may make mistakes all the time in deciding which to use because we focus on the city because it's easiest. It's easier to have kings than it is to have mayors, but we turn the mayor into a king and he's here to have figure heads, celebrities. 'Cause it's hard to do all 50 alderman [of Chicago] and it's hard to do little people who make the system work. So, you pick the representatives of the system and focus on that, but even doing that you just pick one; you don't pick Shaumburg and Lemont and Joliet.

One of the key issues related to proximity in covering news within the city limits in Chicago is balancing coverage between the city's north and south sides. The citywide media have a difficult time attempting to give their whole audience proximate news. By and large, more affluent Whites live on the north side, whereas poorer Blacks live on the south and west sides of the city. Allegations of unequal coverage are lively at WGN. Reporter Roseann Tellez outlines her perspective this way:

Inevitably what happens is the South-side people are the ones that don't get covered. And, you know, I guarantee you if somebody is harmed in any way on the North Shore, it's going to be a big story. So, I have no problem or embarrassment in saying I think we should cover [all fatality stories]. ... Sometimes on the desk they tell me, "No, I don't think we should cover that because I'm sure she was a prostitute." Well that's fine if we're going to start saying, "You know what, we're not going to cover that murder on the North Shore because it was probably a domestic."

The station is aware of the tension this conflict inflicts on its staff and in terms of its coverage. The station's audience is also sensitive to any disparity in coverage between Whites and Blacks. The station receives phone calls when issues of race are indicated in news stories. On one occasion, executive producer Tony Noce said his station's plan for representative coverage backfired. The first year the Chicago Bulls won the National Basketball Association championship, the station sent one of its live trucks to a North-side (White) bar for crowd reaction. The second year the Bulls won, Noce says the staff decided to opt for a South-side (Black) bar:

A lot of Blacks are into basketball, but don't get to the stadium because of the price of tickets or for whatever reason. They go to a lot of these Black bars on the South side to cheer on the Bulls, so what better place than to go there? So we went, but we missed all that stuff on Rush Street where the people went out on the street and went crazy and went bonkers.

The same racial concerns related to the city's geographic makeup are evident at the *Tribune* newsroom. Metro editor Jean Davidson speaks of representative coverage:

We're making a real concerted effort over the last 2 years at least to focus on parts of the city that maybe we've ignored before, in the Black communities, Hispanic communities that aren't necessarily our core readers that you didn't see a lot of in the *Tribune* before, and it wasn't, I don't think, an intentional slightness, that we didn't know what was happening in those communities. We didn't have people out in those communities and ... the [new] diversification of our staff has helped us to cover those.

News staffs at both the *Tribune* and WGN are generally aware that the overall makeup of their audiences is not Black and is not within Chicago's city limits. For example, assistant metro editor Terry Luft says he does his own informal analysis:

> I do empirical [observation] when I'm on the train. I look at the people
> who are reading [*The Chicago Sun Times*] and [those] who are reading
> the *Tribune*. Don't take this the wrong way; you don't see many
> blue-collar [workers] or Blacks or minorities reading the *Tribune*. ...
> And I drive around neighborhoods, especially suburban neighbor-
> hoods and see 10 *Tribune* little plastic carry boxes for every *Sun Times*.

Knowledge about who reads the paper clearly does help shape the
news that is produced. *Tribune* managing editor Dick Ciccone says
his paper is zoned into five different regions, and there are even some
subregional divisions:

> You start to get the northwest suburbs and DuPage and far west
> DuPage suburbs ... there are people there that have absolutely no
> affinity to the city of Chicago and they only want to see Chicago news
> if they can take a perverse joy out of saying, "Thank God I don't live
> there," or if it is really truly significant news or news that can impact
> them. ... We zone our newspaper to the suburbs as much as we can
> and keep the Chicago news restricted to city readers as much as we
> can.

Perceptions of audience clearly play into the news carried in
different issues. For better or worse, that can play into a dispropor-
tionate representation among certain races or stereotyped views. If
reporters know that they are writing to a predominantly White,
suburban audience, that is likely to affect the way they write.
Similarly, if an assignment editor has that understanding, the editor
may choose stories considered more interesting for the White audience in the suburbs.

The *Tribune* does make some effort to avoid Kaniss' city myopia
in terms of its zoning strategy. According to general assignment
reporter Steve Johnson, some think those zoning techniques actually
give too strong a focus to the suburbs in contrast to city coverage:

> I think there is a feeling here that the tide is really turning the other
> way, that the suburbs are really getting their due. There are some
> people who feel that there is just too much emphasis. You know the
> kind of things that will get coverage in the suburbs are really in the
> big picture, minor, compared to the kind of things that will get coverage
> in the city. You'll get a dispute over a liquor license—that will be a big
> story for days in the northwest. Whereas that's going on in Chicago
> neighborhoods every day of the week. ... So, I'm not sure if I agree with

that [a city myopia in reporting] anymore at least here at the *Tribune,* and that's been a definite change in the [last] 7 years.

If Johnson is right, the emphasis on suburban coverage is evidence of a marketing orientation at the paper that heightens the notion of proximity as a news value. The notion that audience members care the most about what happens in their own backyards leads to such an emphasis. Yet, *Tribune* managing editor Dick Ciccone says that the news can never really be local enough for most audience members:

> I was in a focus group once years ago, and the discussion was about "does the *Tribune* cover local news?" And so [one participant] said, "absolutely not." And the guy said "Well look at yesterday's *Tribune.* It had a story about Harold Washington [Chicago's former mayor]. ... Well, that's not local." ... "Well, what's local news do you think?" "Well, the burglary at the hardware store right down the block—that wasn't in the *Tribune.* They do a terrible job of covering local news." But that's what most readers think local news is: What has happened on my street is local. Everything else is somebody else's news.

In this case, Ciccone's image of his audience has been shaped by formal analysis—a focus group. Yet, he often disputes the formal answer, preferring to focus on the news product rather than on audience preferences. He bases his decisions about proximity and other news values on his own wisdom, gained from years of experience in working with news:

> So, how do you satisfy all those readers? Well, the way I know you don't satisfy them is listening to focus groups and readership surveys. You have to put out a paper that has a good consistent philosophy about what it is you're going to try to do everyday.

At WGN, assignment editor Dave Jaffe refers to understanding about how far out [geographically] viewer interest goes as the "mystical area of news judgment ... [based on] a certain number of years in the business and simply ... knowing which story is better than another story." Media scholar John Merrill (Dennis & Merrill, 1984) made reference to this kind of knowing-in-action:

> [Today's editor] uses intuition, instinct, and perceptions of news value stemming from experience and common sense. Often, also, he projects

his own likes and dislikes about news to his readers. This may not be
scientific, but it is useful and quick—and it works well. (p. 146)

At times, notions of proximity and the implicit audience that
supports them take a back seat to the realities of news production.
Jaffe provides evidence of Kaniss' city myopia and Fishman's practical accomplishment perspective when arguing that news from
farther out in the metropolitan area may be substituted with stories
that are more easily gathered:

> There are a number of criteria [used to determine which stories are
> covered]. One of them is, can we get this story and get it back and get
> it on the air?—the sheer physical question. Is it possible for us to do
> it? If not, and it's a good story, ... how can we get it? Is there another
> station nearby that can get it and send it to us? Is there a stringer out
> that way who can cover it and get it back here? ... A faraway story that
> is pretty good will fall by the wayside if we have several close-up stories
> that are real good.

The *Tribune*'s Ciccone and WGN's Jaffe have recognized the im-
possibility of giving every reader the news of what is happening on
their own street and covering every story regardless of how many
miles it is away from the news hub. A newspaper or television station
simply does not have the capability or necessary resources for covering all locales.

Still, the editors believe that their audience is most attracted to
news that happens nearby. Because zoning is a possibility for the
newspaper, it is a clear strategy used to attract the suburban reader.
WGN, which must cater to all viewers at the same time, is more likely
to rely on stories in Chicago because they are easier to gather and
represent the largest single block of viewers in contrast to any one
suburban locale.

CONFLICT

When news people talk about the news value of conflict, they typically are referring to a tension between two clear sides—a tension
that fits well into their precepts of objectivity. They will typically seek
out spokespersons from each side of a dispute to structure the story
(Berkowitz & Beach, 1993). Journalists perceive that the conflict
they structure also exists in the world of their overall audience. They
see that as both an asset and a liability. As an asset, journalists
believe that with greater conflict comes greater interest in a story.

Therefore, at times, conflict is used, and the dramatic elements of a story are heightened to entice audience interest. Conflict is occasionally viewed as divisive, and journalists believe they must be especially careful and clearly nonpartisan so as not to alienate audience members. WGN assignment editor Mike Kertez spoke about audience reaction to his station's reporting:

> People tell us when we do something wrong, I don't mean 5 minutes after the show ends, I mean 2 minutes after the piece ends and you can always tell the nature of the call. I mean we get lots of screwballs, and we get lots of people like Democrats who don't like Republicans. Republicans who don't like Democrats. Abortionists who don't like antiabortionists and all that kind of stuff.

Such perceptions of audience reaction heighten the importance conflict plays in the newsroom as a news value. In some instances, audience is viewed as strongly divided and, inherently, strongly interested in a topic. *Tribune* reporter Steve Johnson recounted such a story:

> I think the other time when you think of an audience is when you know there's an interest group really concerned about what you're writing about. The gun story is a perfect example. I very much had it in my mind that if there's a mistake, [if] there is something unfair, I'm going to have the NRA [National Rifle Association] or the opposite side, the antihandgun side, jumping down my throat the next day. So I think that's when you definitely have an audience in mind.

In stories that entail conflict, reporters voice clear concerns about the audience. They often view the audience as clearly divided into the two sides they present in their story. Notions of conflict also build a sense of the dramatic. In his text, *News Reporting and Writing,* Mencher (1994) equated conflict with drama:

> Conflict: Events that reflect clashes between people or institutions. Strife, antagonism and confrontation have provided stories since people drew pictures of the hunt on the walls of their caves. The struggles of people with themselves and their gods, a Hamlet or a Prometheus, are the essentials of drama. The contemporary counterparts are visible to the journalist whose eye is trained to see the dramatic. (pp. 52–53)

When Illinois Governor Jim Edgar offered his annual budget to the state on March 3, 1993, the front-page *Tribune* story focused on the element of conflict between competing sides. Reporter R. Pearson portrayed the conflict as highly dramatic:

> Springfield—Gov. Jim Edgar used his third annual budget address Wednesday to portray himself as an education-minded governor heading into next year's campaign.
>
> But Democrats, who hope to take over the governor's mansion in 1994 for the first time in 16 years, would have none of it. They accused Edgar of breaking his campaign promise not to raise taxes and said he would force the state's towns to raise taxes as well.
>
> The stage is now set for a long and bitter confrontation between Republicans led by Edgar and new Senate President James "Pate" Philip and Democrats headed by House Speaker Michael Madigan and Chicago Mayor Richard Daley.

This story type sets up the journalist as storyteller and the audience as spectator with clear, definable sides in something akin to an athletic event. The journalist uses drama and a sense of conflict to add interest for the reader.

One of the most compelling forms of conflict is that of "good versus evil," especially when the journalist is implicitly portrayed as the "good guy" bringing the "bad guy" to light. Such was the story that WGN anchor/reporter Steve Sanders recounted as a story of which he was especially proud:

> Father and son movers ... this began with what we thought was a routine consumer story, your basic television consumer rip-off story on how a local moving company was taking advantage of customers. What they were doing was moving their furniture, then essentially refusing to unload the truck unless the customer came up with another $400 or $500, $600 dollars in cash—holding the furniture hostage, in essence. It was a good story; [we] did it. In fact we did two parts on it.

The story is compelling because it has clear sides: the journalist working on behalf of Chicago area victims, and the illegal movers. What heightened the story value for Sanders and his audience is the dramatic quality he painted behind the conflict:

> After the first night, [we] got a call from a Florida investigator who was watching us on cable [televison] who said, "That fellow you interviewed, you know he's chief suspect in the murder of a federal

witness in a mob trial in Miami." The reason he's in Chicago was because they moved him up here as a payback, and they wanted to—until the heat goes off—they wanted to get him out of Miami. Twenty-six year-old kid—pretty young to be running a pretty good sized moving company. So we continued to follow the story.

Notice how the sides are set: journalist working as public advocate and the crime family endangering the public. Not only does this build the journalist's credibility with his audience, but it adds to the dramatic quality of conflict:

Then we found out there was a nationwide network of father-and-son moving companies—all controlled, we're told, by the Lucchesi crime family out of New York. Owned by a guy name John Vicaro. In Miami, Orlando, Atlanta, New York–New Jersey area, Chicago, and Los Angeles, just to name a few cities. And in almost every one of those cities, they have piled up a record number of complaints. So, we continued to follow the story. It resulted in a number of hearings at the Illinois commerce commission. ... To make a long story short, they took the license away and shut 'em down.

The conflict has resolution. Good prevails over evil, right over wrong. Still, the journalist allows for one last bit of tension as he finishes his story:

... and in what we thought to be a somewhat unusual procedure, the Chicago judge granted them temporary authority to continue operating until he could hear an appeal of the ICC [Illinois Commerce Commission] decision. That was a fun story. ... We got an unbelievable number of calls.

Audience response contributes to the journalist's understanding that such a story works.

The journalist as *watchdog* also presents a clear conflict between two sides. A picture of the journalist uncovering wrongdoing is offered by *Tribune* reporter Bill Recktenwald:

There's a Pulitzer prize sitting in the glass panel out front here that was given to the *Tribune* for its vote fraud investigation. People now can regularly go in and vote in private in Chicago. I can remember when that wouldn't happen. ... The *Tribune* started the thing, and time and time again Bill Jones and I worked on ambulances back in the [19]70s and abuses were found. ... And as a result, people got indicted for giving poor care and taking bribes and all sorts of terrible things.

In this story type, the journalist works as ally and advocate for the audience. Implicit is the assumption that the audience appreciates and welcomes such reporting. The story type is reminiscent of the muckraking era of journalism (Emery & Emery, 1988):

The struggle between big business and workers and farmers was as old as the struggle between the Hamiltonians and the Jeffersonians for control of the government. ... Joining hands with politicians and labor leaders, reformers and agitators, professors and ministers, social workers and philanthropists, the men and women of journalism and literature helped to shape the course of the great crusade. (p. 250)

As the journalist joins forces with the audience, the conflict is reinforced in a them-versus-us dynamic: bad guys versus good guys.

When audience members react to the stories with their letters, phone calls, and tales of personal experiences, the story type is reinforced. In turn, repeatedly producing this type of story reinforces a vision of the audience as occasional victim and more often as avid spectator. When journalists produce these stories of conflict, they reaffirm their notion that audiences, too, are captivated by the conflict.

PROMINENCE

Certain individuals help to elevate "happenings" to "news" status because those individuals are deemed to hold special significance for audience members. People become significant for the audience when they are viewed to have personal impact for the audience or, more likely, when they can be symbolically tied to news consumers. The prominent individual often is symbolic for the audience because he or she is seen to represent a significant group or even an entire community. Carey (1986), for example, argued that American journalism begins with the question, "Who?":

The primary subject of journalism is people—what they say and do. Moreover, the subject is usually an individual—what someone says and does. Groups, in turn, are usually personified by leaders or representatives. ... Because news is mainly about the doings and sayings of individuals, [the question of] why is usually answered by identifying the motives of those individuals. (p. 180)

Journalism texts invariably list prominence as a key news value. Strentz (1989) argued that some sources can "make" news, even without real cause: "Well-established sources may also be sought for comment on tangential issues. And a source that has really 'arrived' may be asked for comment on issues and events that he or she knows nothing about" (p. 105).

However, prominence need not refer only to famous people, but also to those who represent large constituencies or organizations. Strentz (1989) argued that news sources who are able to effectively speak out on an issue will be called again by reporters looking for a representative quote. Hohenberg (1960) suggested that prominence takes on added significance when it can be shown to have impact on the audience:

Names by themselves do not make news; otherwise, newspapers would resemble telephone books and city directories. Something has to happen to make news of a name, and the importance of the news varies in direct proportion to the meaning that the event has for the community (p. 262).

Tribune editor Dick Ciccone concedes that stories of major significance will often be highlighted by personalities but argues that prominence is not such a strong news value for his paper. He again uses his paper's coverage of Boris Yeltsin and the Russian Republic as indicative:

I think if you go back over the past 18 months, you'll find so many of the stories about him are on the insides of newspapers, not on the front because even though he's a well-known figure, nothing was happening that was threatening.

Ciccone also contends that not all stories have clear personalities that represent differing sides: "We deal with Bosnia as a conflict, as a tragedy of nationalism. We have no personalities there, we're not even sure there are good guys or bad guys, but that's a conflict."

Still, Ciccone charges that his broadcast rivals do highlight prominence to tell their stories. He also acknowledges that his newspaper will play up a prominent figure when that figure has clear relevance for his audience:

I put the resignation of [former National Football League (NFL)
Commissioner] Pete Roselle on the front page of the newspaper, 5 [or]
6 years ago ... because what I felt that Pete Roselle did in crafting the
television deal of the 1960s changed the way America lived. Little boys
did not get taken to the zoo or did not get taken out in the park to bat
at balls between noon and 6 from September to December after Pete
Roselle put together the deal that had CBS and NBC giving in to
football games every Sunday afternoon. Now by the 1990s, a whole
generation grew up with an overwhelming amount of televised sport.

In this case, a perception of personal impact and knowledge about
his audience caused the news chief to play up prominence. Ciccone
would argue that prominence is a key news value when the figure
has personal relevance for the reading audience. Roselle is prominent because he has had real impact on the audience.

As illustrated in chapter 2, another sports personality who received great coverage in Chicago during the observation period for
this research (October 1992–March 1993) was the Chicago Bears'
head coach, Mike Ditka. WGN-TV dedicated 15 minutes of its hour-
long newscast at 9:00 p.m. to the story of his firing. Its noon newscast
also heavily played up the stories of Ditka's termination and the
hiring of a new coach. The day's noon producer, Tim Jackson explains:

There's a tremendous amount of money that goes into it [professional
football], and there's a tremendous amount of conversation that backs
it up. Or, you could convert that and say there is a tremendous amount
of popular conversation that's backed up by a tremendous amount of
money being spent on that. We have scores, not dozens, scores of bars
that are driven by our football team and our baseball teams. We have
scores [of] NFL or league teams sporting shops. ... I find that amazing.
... So, we axed Mike Ditka. Who's Mike Ditka? Mike Ditka is a
personality that some people believe is beyond realm.

The news producer makes the case that football has a great impact
on the city and therefore the story of Ditka's firing becomes more
newsworthy. Yet, clearly, something more is operating. Ditka serves
as a symbolic figure for Chicago, "a personality that some people
believe is beyond realm." Carey (1986) argued that individuals serve
as a personification of a group. Ditka served as personification of
WGN's viewing audience. Jackson continues:

It's really a statement about the people of Chicago and the way that
they support and are loyalists to—once they decide that they like you,

once that they decide that you are a member of their family, whether you turn on the herd and go in the other direction, ... they're going to stay with you ... until you really rub them the wrong way. And boy they stuck by the Bears.

Ditka had therefore become more than a symbol of the Bears; he had become a symbol for Chicago. As the audience identified with the Bears, they identified with Ditka. Therefore, justification for the lengthy treatment of the story is based on notions of audience. Prominence is played up because the audience is assumed to identify with the character in some way. Roselle is prominent because of his impact on audience members' lives. Ditka is prominent because audience members have learned to care about him.

Prominence as an audience concern becomes a given assumption. These journalists assume that the audience is interested in prominent figures when those figures can be shown to have either a direct or a symbolic impact on the audience.

CONCLUSION

Notions of audience are a tacit part of these news factors. A perception that the audience is increasingly using competitive media for discovering the news has changed the way these news workers see timeliness. Workers at modern news organizations understand that there are now faster modes of discovering the news than the traditional morning newspaper or evening newscast. Therefore, the news workers seek to offer their audiences something more. For the broadcast journalist, the goal is to give the very latest details and the pictures that go with it. If possible, the best coverage is providing a live report. For the print journalist, the goal is to provide the full story, with depth that other news media cannot provide.

Proximity takes on a new meaning given varying understandings of the audience. Knowledge that the audience has a very localized interest leads the newspaper to focus on zoning its coverage to particular areas. A belief that the audience is better served with more sophisticated news gathering equipment leads broadcasting professionals to serve up the news from new angles at new locations—to give the aura of "omnipresence." The knowledge by city news workers that their audiences are more suburban than urban and more White than Black undoubtedly has some bearing on which areas are covered and how they are covered.

The belief that notions of conflict are engaging for the audience teaches the news gatherer to look for that tension in the news. A state's budget proposal becomes the catalyst for a story that focuses on the in-fighting between Republicans and Democrats. Conflict seems inherently tied to implicit notions of drama because the drama is viewed to further engage the audience.

Elements of prominence are elevated when the figures can be shown to represent groups or when they are believed to have personal relevance for large portions of the news audience. Prominent figures play a symbolic role because audience members have come to know and identify with them; they have become especially pertinent because they are a part of popular culture with which audience members are keenly familiar.

These four news values are clearly large elements of the modern news equation. They are shaped by images of the audience. Although much of the discussion related to these four news values is predicated on concerns for the audience, it is clear that sometimes these discussions serve merely as a justification for what news organizations choose to crank out as the news product. As WGN assignment editor Dave Jaffe stated, a primary consideration is actually, "Can we get this story and get it back and get it on the air?" The key consideration is directed toward "manufacturing" the news product—how feasible is it to get the story on the air or in the paper?

Two other newsworthiness factors, impact and interest, are perhaps the most clearly related to news workers' perceptions of their audiences. As such, they become very important and act, at times, as "master" (see chapter 4) values. Impact and interest as they are related to what journalists deem to be important are the focus of the following chapter.

Chapter 4

The Tacit Audience in the "Master" News Values: Interest, Importance, and Impact

The last two news values considered by Itule and Anderson (1987) in their reporting text, *News Writing and Reporting for Today's Media,* are *impact* and *interest,* the two news values perhaps most closely linked to the audience. When journalists think about tailoring their copy to their audience, they very often focus on these two news values. Yet when they consider their overall goals for their work, what Schön (1983) termed *reflecting-in-action,* they often turn to another value: *importance.* A broader goal for working journalists is to share with their audience what they deem to be important for them. The important story, however, is not always inherently of immediate interest for news consumers. Therefore, journalists look for strategies for making the important story interesting. Very typically, the key strategy employed revolves around the news value *impact.* The journalist works to make the important story interesting by showing personal impact for the audience. Due to their elevated rank in news organizations, these three news values (interest, impact, and importance) function with a kind of "master value" status. The interplay between the three news values is illustrated, for example, in the selection of a lead news story for WGN's noon newscast. Assistant news director Jim Disch describes the choice between two stories considered for the lead:

> The two lead stories yesterday were Sears, the catalog, 50,000 layoffs nationwide—quite a substantial story with a lot of economic impact obviously, ... and the other major story in my mind, at least at 12 noon,

was still the CIA shooting. ... Some crazy outside the CIA building in Washington is walking up to cars and shooting people. Killed two people, injured a couple of others and then disappeared into the crowd.

Disch argues that his station's decision to lead with the Sears story was right because it "affected the most people." The story is seen to be *important* because of its widespread economic impact:

I guess what story affects your audience the most—that's probably the most basic question you can ask of any lead story. It affects you because it hits you in the pocket book. ... You might know someone who works at Sears. If not, you might be in one of the communities where a Sears store is closing down and even [on] a more superficial level, if one company can lay off 50,000 people, there must be something not quite right with the economy.

The second story in Disch's newscast is seen to be *interesting*. The scene is something out of a violent thriller. There is the CIA, a mad gunman, and innocent victims. But, just as in the Sears story, there is a sense of social importance as well. One might wonder, if a mad gunman can go around shooting people right outside the CIA building, is anyone safe? Disch continues:

The other one we started with doesn't affect people as much, the CIA story, but sometimes a story is worth the lead ... just because of the intrigue. I mean some idiot just walking up and just starting to blow holes in people; I mean, they were in their cars. They were driving in this area, and someone just started taking shots and then disappeared. ... So, there is a lot of intrigue in that story.

The news boss sees the two stories as very compelling; one has great economic significance, whereas the other generates great interest. Both considerations are audience centered. Not only is he talking about providing his readers with what they *want* to know, he is also hoping to provide them with what they *ought* to know. Disch is touching upon an inherent tension between journalists' professional values and their notion that they must, in some way, appeal to the audience—a marketing orientation.

In the discussion of interest and impact that follows, I also examine the notion of importance, the third master value. I argue that while interest clearly is tied to a marketing orientation, importance most clearly reflects journalists' professional values. Journalists use impact as a means for tying interest and importance together, that is, as a means for resolving the tension between professional values that prompt them to tell their audience what they *ought* to know and a marketing orientation that prompts them to tell their audience what they *want* to know.

TENSION BETWEEN INTEREST AND IMPORTANCE

Chicago Tribune metro editor Jean Davidson describes the kind of effect she would like her stories to have on her readers, cognizant of the realities of modern newspaper readership trends:

> I think that we are competing for a small slice of our readers' day. ... I would like to produce stories that are both interesting and when it is appropriate, prompt people to thought and to action about specific issues. I think that appropriateness is the key. Sometimes [stories are] going to be flip and funny and they'll belong on page 1 just because they're a good read, and others are a serious critical examination of important issues.

Davidson points to two competing concerns facing her reporters and, for that matter, every reporter: Do they focus on *interesting and entertaining* their audience or do they focus on what they deem to be *important and necessary* for their audience? The question may be rephrased by the journalist simply as, "Do I give them what they want, or do I give them what they need?" This is the heart of the tension between professional values and a marketing orientation to the news.

Traditional professional values place the journalist at the forefront of deciding which stories need to be told. Squires (1993) began his book by focusing on Lippman's view of the press as "the beam of searchlight that moved restlessly about bringing one episode and then another out of the darkness into vision" (p. 3). Lavine and Wackman (1988) characterized the view as flowing from

> ... an awareness of social responsibility by editors, reporters, screen writers, and other message producers. They felt that it was their job to decide what society should read or see. Judgments of that sort involved their expertise and integrity as professionals and they were

loath to share that responsibility and power, even with the citizens for whom they were preparing a message. (p. 254)

A marketing orientation, on the other hand, puts the audience at the forefront. Lavine and Wackman (1988) characterized this alternative perspective: "This approach, which was developed in the last 20 to 30 years, concentrates primary attention on consumers. ... Media firms began to identify customers' needs and desires first; then they tailored news ... to match consumer interests" (p. 253).

Typically, today's journalists offer a mix of what they see as important and what they think their audiences will find to be either interesting or of immediate use. When they focus on impact, they often are providing information that is important and interesting at the same time. As most journalists compare the three master values —interest, importance, and impact—they see a bit of a balancing act. They want to both engage their audience and also tell them what they ought to know.

INTEREST

Interest is the news value most closely associated with a marketing orientation. Journalists make mention of it often enough that it clearly functions as a master value. Oftentimes other news values are couched in terms of interest. For example, proximate news is considered of greater value because it is assumed that audience members will be more interested in news that happens near them.

Interest has traditionally been a key component in any list of news values. In White's (1950) classic "The Gate Keeper" study, the newspaper editor who was studied rejected more than 100 items because they were either "not interesting" or of "no interest" (p. 386). Itule and Anderson's (1987) text focused on the emotional appeal of human interest stories. Interest for them is the quality that can lead a reader or viewer into the story being told. Equating interest with what she called the "sexiness quotient," Kaniss (1991) argued that "The journalist's fundamental job is to create interest—for himself, for his editors, and ultimately for his audience" (p. 86). Yet, as exemplified at both WGN and *The Chicago Tribune,* interest can take on a myriad of different meanings: gore, unusualness, suspense, celebrity, and so forth.

The noon news producer at WGN television, Forrest Respess, has been in the news business for 45 years and puts great emphasis on interesting his audience. He is a firm believer in the notion that "grabbing" his viewer is a prominent, if not *the* prominent goal behind his work. He unabashedly espouses a market-driven formula for news:

> A lot of my colleagues disagree with me on this, but regardless, our newscasts are still a part of show biz and you've got to have something that is going to attract, that's going to make them want to listen or watch. If you don't do that, you could have the most journalistic[ally] perfect story in the world, but if it doesn't have any appeal, if it doesn't have the element that makes the guy out there want to hear the story, forget it. This is show biz, whether you like it or not. Without the audience, you might as well fold up and go home. You've got to play. You don't want to compromise your principles, your ethics, but you've got to think the way they think out there, and say, "If I was out there and I was not a journalist, would I want to watch this story?"

Respess raises the argument that interest is required to maintain an audience. No interest, no viewers. Without viewers there is no chance for a news show to survive, much less tell the audience what they need to know. He makes passing reference to professional values, "You don't want to compromise your principles, your ethics"—but he clearly sees interest as the predominant news value. Therefore, he attempts to build interest into each newscast:

> I think [viewers] like to see the action. It's playing to the more base emotions. ... If you've got a good, if you want to call it "good," a very significant fire with people injured or jumping out of windows, what have you, or a particularly graphic accident of some kind ... What's the first thing people look at in the newspaper? Obituaries. They look at obituaries. And it's a grabber. I don't care who you are. You're sitting here and looking off to the side and all of a sudden in the corner of your eye you see flames or something like that on the television set, you're going to look at that television set. It's a grabber. It's appealing to the more basic instincts of your audience.

Interest is a key concern in the television newsroom, but it is hard to define. Typically, journalists do not provide formal theories of audience interest, but they provide lists of interesting topics. In other words, journalists know stories that work—and stories that don't. They know product image. Tacit audience image flows out of product image. Journalists develop an understanding of audience through trial and error. They develop an understanding of what will and will not interest their audience by doing a set of stories over and over again. For example, some WGN reporters disagree with their producers and assignment editors over the coverage of fatal accidents. One reporter put it this way:

> We sometimes air single car accidents with video. ... I absolutely can't stand that. Chicago's 20 times bigger than [the market in which I used to work]. We didn't do single car accidents down there—fatals. ... The reason [we air them here] is that we've got these stringers now who will go out and shoot this stuff overnight. ... In Chicago, any night there are probably three or four fatal car accidents. ... It drives me nuts, and I don't think it's that newsworthy. ... I really don't think viewers care about it, even if it's good video. ...

Working with the same material can, at times, lead two news workers to opposite conclusions about what really interests their news audience. The reporter concludes that the repetition of the news accident bores the viewer, whereas the producer focuses on the interest generated from crushed metal and fiery blazes. But although conclusions may differ, both conclusions are based on experience with this sort of story.

Some stories are simply recognized as interesting because they are filled with action. An example of a story that would meet WGN's noon producer's tacit understanding of the audience as interested in action and gore was the station's next-day coverage of an accident at Chicago's O'Hare International Airport on March 28, 1992. An automobile jumped a sidewalk and killed one man and injured several others. The story featured pictures of ambulances, blood on the sidewalk, the opened air bag of an auto, a shot of a body in an ambulance, and the following graphic depiction of the scene by a witness:

> It was pretty messy. I mean, it was people lying all over the floor. And you know, there was a lot of blood from a couple of people here. There was one gentleman—I know two of them had broken legs for sure. ... The guy that got hit—he was on top of the hood and then the car ran him over, the van ran him over. I think that was how the body got so twisted up, when the car ran him over ... because his head was all twisted out of shape.

This is a clear example of the kind of story Respess espouses. It seems to work so well because it has the elements that the news producer says he believes are essential for captivating an audience.

For him, gore is interesting: "It's a grabber ... appealing to the more basic instincts." The report later includes reference to a similar accident at Chicago's O'Hare Airport 1 year ago. Although once a protective barrier had been considered, no corrective action had been taken. Therefore, the journalist seems to have a rationale for the "blood 'n guts" reporting. The journalist is, in fact, warning the public about possible danger. The story has both interest and importance.

Respess goes on to argue that gory wrecks have their place:

> If you have a particularly gory wreck where drunk driving was involved, things like that, I'm a strong believer in doing that—in showing those things if there's alcohol involved or drugs involved—in showing what can happen.

The journalist is able to argue for "blood 'n guts" by tying interest to importance ("Look what can be the result of driving drunk. Look what can happen if you're not careful.") On occasion, audience interest is used as justification for printing sensational material in the newspaper. *Tribune* assistant metro editor Kerry Luft talks about readers' interest in the coverage of the Branch Davidian cult exposed in Waco, Texas, in February 1993. He echoes much of the same kind of rhetoric used by WGN's Respess:

> It's just a weird enough story where people have a prurient interest in it; you want to read. It's got cults, it's got shoot 'em up ... there's just something viscerally in us that makes us want to read that story. That's why the *National Enquirer* has a bigger circulation than any daily newspaper in the country.... That's why those tabloids sell. They're stories that people like to read about. They're blood and guts. ... There's just something inside you.

Both Respess and Luft see "blood 'n guts" reporting as compelling and inherently of interest to their audience. Interest is also characterized at times by intrigue. In such a scenario, a good story is like a good crime or detective novel. It has characters, drama, and conflict. Assignment editor Mike Kertez talked about one such story that demonstrated Hitchcockian suspense:

> Some really interesting stories are intricate like the one today where we had a stalker in court on a misdemeanor and a real complex case,

[where he beat] his wife severely and then went to jail and wrote threatening letters saying when he got out of jail, he was going to kill her. When he did get out of jail, they rearrested him on the threatening letters, but the stalker law says that you have to have two specific instances where he was in the vicinity.

Having introduced his characters and the inherent tension, the editor then provides the news peg by which he is able to tell his story today:

Now his case is coming up and will be finished today, and the problem with him is they really don't have any reason to keep him in court on those charges for more than another month. ... They tried to get him to plead guilty to the charge, put him on electronic surveillance where at least they can monitor where he was, but he wouldn't accept that; he's willing to do an extra month or two in jail just so he can get out and kill his wife. Now that has all the elements of being a great story.

The assignment editor could argue that such a story might prompt his viewers to challenge the specifics of the current state stalking law that allows this man to prey on his wife—or at least prompt them to become alarmed. Instead, he focuses on the elements of the story that prompt audience interest. Clearly, that concern for appealing to audience interest is deeply imbedded in the television news room.

Newspapers certainly are also not unaware of the need to interest readers but, one does hear less talk in terms of simply "grabbing" reader interest in the *Tribune* newsroom. Instead of talking about interest, the key phrase bantered around the room is a "good read." This refers to a story that is compelling and engaging. Metro editor Jean Davidson defines a good read this way:

A story that could be a long story but you don't realize it was a long story until you're done. You're just drawn quickly through it. It's an interesting, original, fresh look at something that isn't necessarily original or new, just a story that is very engaging.

During a morning news meeting, a suburban editor talks about a story he has assigned that should meet the definition of a good read:

So, I'm going to have (writers) put together a piece that is kind of a reader about how this town, Woodstock, which is probably most noted for being the home of the most famous crime-fighter ever, Dick Tracy, is reacting to the idea of the police chief being turned in on indictment for eavesdropping. So, I think that has potential for being a nice little reader ... how they're going to be turned in tomorrow, surrendering on those charges.

This story takes on added value because the editor has a special angle by which he can grab his audience.

WGN weekend anchor and reporter Roseann Tellez says the question of what will interest an audience is sometimes explicitly discussed among her colleagues:

> We do debate that. ... We go back and forth over what we think people will be interested in. But you just have to bring more people into the conversation and see what kind of consensus there is. ... The other thing, too, is just what everybody is talking about. We all kind of know what everybody is talking about out there.

"What everybody is talking about" is another common response to the question, "What is news?" or "What is interesting?" Predominantly, in the television newsroom, the job of identifying what people are talking about or what might interest them is the domain of the assignment desk. Mike Kertez is the morning slot man and assignment editor at WGN. He contends that his job is to appeal to a variety of interests:

> You try to get as many stories as you can that have as wide a range of interest to people, both in their lives and what they perceive [of] as the world. You also try to cover the daily events of life. It may not be important, like Madonna's *Sex* book coming out on the market. In the realm of things, those aren't important events, but those are little road maps on the way—little things that happened.... Even those which are ... silly. You try to chronicle what's happening, both socially and in sports and in other fields. You try to cover major things that people have interest in ... plus those incidents, happenstance, like people shot, day-to-day events that make news.

The assignment editor suggests that the audience has a natural curiosity about a range of topics and the news organization's job is, more or less, to offer up a pallet of stories to keep their appetites for news whetted. The assignment editor can provide a list of stories that he believes are interesting, and in that list he reflects assumptions about his audience. The assignment editor knows product image. From the news product and the array of stories he assigns, he comes to believe that those types of stories are inherently interesting for his audience.

Although all news organizations are susceptible to the desire to appeal to their audience's "more basic instincts," organizations that spend much of their time on these types of stories are usually labeled "sensationalistic." In Chicago, the CBS affiliate WBBM-TV, Channel 2, had recently taken such an approach and many throughout the Chicago news industry were critical. WGN executive producer, Tony Noce, characterizes the approach taken at his CBS rival:

> They, right now, are going in for the spectacular—crime, very visual kinds of stories, whether they be local or not, any kind of train crash, plane crash, flood—even if it's way out anywhere. ... Now with satellite, you can be local anywhere, and you can send your guy there to make it local because your guy is there ... sexy stories, animal stories, crime stories—that short attention span. I'm going to hit you with images very quickly just to keep you focused, not so much understanding the story, but just keeping-you-interested-for-the-moment kind of story.

The implicit message verbalized by Noce is that Channel 2 has gone overboard in a market-driven perspective and has retreated from journalism's basic professional values—telling the audience what they ought to know. Generally, workers at WGN feel that their own newscasts are more responsible than those at Channel 2. Still, employees like WGN writer/producer Tim Jackson concede to their own desires to keep their news show entertaining:

> One of the regular pieces of feedback we get about our broadcasts here at Channel 9 is that we're just regular and that we don't hype too much. ... I think you do the best that you can to make it interesting. The conservative side of me gets a little nervous when I say, "Gee, is that exciting." And at the same time, the producer side of me and the Aaron Spelling part of me as a producer says, "You bet I want it exciting. Boy, I want the top of this show to be like a water-slide ride with jet engines on it. And I want to keep these people glued to this box." So I've got a parallax of views.

That "parallax of views" again points to the implicit tension between the journalist's professional values and a marketing perspective to the news. It highlights why some stories are believed to merit more coverage than others.

One story that received enormous media coverage in Chicago in 1992 was the murder of Tammy Zywicki, an area college student murdered on her way back to college. Assignment editor Dave Jaffe explained why the story seemed to merit so much coverage in comparison with other murder stories:

> Better story. There are 970 murders [in the Chicago area in a year]. We cover, maybe 60 ... a drive-by shooting in a bad neighborhood. We have a grocery store owner who the neighborhood loved and was slain. Or if we have a kid walking to school, in front of the school and he's shot by a sniper ... that focuses people's attention. Or, if we have a girl who is missing, took a drive, and her parents contact all the media, contact all the authorities, set up news conferences, set up news trees of all the friends, get the information out, distribute flyers, get searches going at colleges and at local high schools. It's going to get more attention. It's made a bigger story, a lot more coverage.

Notice how Jaffe bases his argument about coverage on notions of the audience when he says, "That focuses people's attention." The editor who determines story assignments from a marketing perspective will undoubtedly judge some stories as more meritorious because they naturally attract audience interest. The reporter who bases his or her assessments about coverage on "fairness" and operates from the perspective of her professional values will see the proper selection of stories differently. Sometimes this tension between these values creates conflict within the organization. For example, one reporter and anchorperson voiced a clear marketing perspective that contradicted the perspective of the producer:

> I have a continuing disagreement with my producer. I don't think that the fighting in Bosnia-Herzegovina is first segment news every day. He does. He's 25 years older than I am. He's been in the business for 50 years—probably harks back to the time when there was a greater emphasis on international news. I came from an environment where if you didn't have an audience, there was a good chance you didn't have a job.

When facing conflict, journalists in these news organizations often learn to couch their arguments in terms of the balance between interest and importance. For example, assignment editor Mike Kertez explains how one story was approached:

> Today people were overcome by [fumes from] a school furnace; nobody [was] seriously hurt. I hate stories like that, because I find nothing interesting. However, if there are a lot of kids in school, producers like [these stories] because they can go to the hospital and there are all those kids. Producers tend to like stories like that; they're interesting visually. ... I've argued about overcome stories at least 40 or 50 times, and I always say there was nobody seriously hurt. ... The producer will say, "It's a school; there are a lot of kids involved. Maybe we could talk about other issues like faulty furnaces. ... " And we go through this little battle and one side wins.

The assignment editor argues that the story will not interest his audience because no one was injured. He bases that judgment on his own level of interest in the story. The producer finds the story attractive because he believes that the visuals will work to attract an audience—to lead them into the story. He also appeals to the assignment editor's belief that the story is not inherently interesting (because no one was injured) by suggesting that the story could be expanded to address other issues. He also appeals to professional values of importance, arguing that the news staff might include a discussion of faulty furnaces.

As the preceding examples suggest, journalists find a range of topics interesting because of what they perceive will attract an audience. Interest has been equated as something that is a "grabber" and appeals to the "more basic instincts." It has been thought of as "conflict" and "intrigue," as "compelling" and "entertaining." It has been characterized by topics that "everybody is talking about" and that "people will read." It has been considered the "events of the times." Ironic detail and good writing are thought to be interesting. Finally, interest is defined as personal and "personally relevant." Its meaning is seemingly as varied as the people who work in news organizations.

Thus, although the concept of interest has not been clearly defined by the news professionals, journalists do have an understanding about what they and their audience will find interesting. That knowledge is based on their years of experience in developing those stories. On occasion, there may be differences among news workers regarding what will interest an audience. Those differences will lead to different ideas about which stories to cover and how to cover them.

The difference in perspectives is typically subtle and sometimes careful scrutiny is needed to distinguish them from each other. For instance, merely by referring to this station's news presentation as a "show," a producer indicates his understanding that he needs to entertain his audience. Yet, when he talks about a "conservative side," he undoubtedly refers to his own professional values that suggest that his primary job is not to entertain his viewers but to inform them about what his news team deems important.

IMPORTANCE

Importance, although not listed by Itule and Anderson (1987) as one of their key news values, clearly plays a key role for journalists in helping them define what is news. It is the news value most closely aligned with a professional values orientation and, therefore, focuses as a master value in and of itself. Like interest, however, there are a good variety of ideas about what is important. It is often tied to governmental activity; at other times it is equated with exposing wrongdoing.

Although journalists and journalism organizations are clearly cognizant of the need to sell papers or earn ratings points, many, if not most, are motivated by the notion that what they are doing is not only generating important information for their audience, but is also serving a vital responsibility for the greater society. Media scholar Everette Dennis (Dennis & Merrill, 1984) wrote:

> Journalism is, in fact, engaged in a public service—the free flow of information and ideas is at the core of First Amendment freedom in the United States. The press has special protection under the Constitution, not simply to allow newspaper and broadcast owners to make a profit, but because as a matter of law and social policy we believe that a free press is essential to a functioning democracy. (p. 156)

The notion of importance conveys different images to different journalists but reflects their professional orientation about what they are all about. They are acting as a watchdog on government, telling the public what they need to know about government and large organizations. By telling what is important, the press serves as public servant to its audience. Hough (1995) wrote, "Without knowledge of public affairs—of the management of our government, of economic matters, of cultural and social phenomena—people would find it difficult not only to vote intelligently but to manage their own lives" (p. 182). Sometimes reporters and editors, motivated by professional values, say they believe they need to present information because it is important, although definitely not interesting, to most of the audience. At *The Chicago Tribune,* Davidson contends that her paper's duty to "chronicle" events may be an interest turn-off for her readers:

> We are the paper of public record so there are some stories that are like oatmeal; they're not terribly interesting. ... We have to cover every development in utility rate cases, and I think there is a real hard-core readership for those stories and most other people read the headlines and the first paragraph and wouldn't be caught dead reading the rest. And I say this as someone who covered the Illinois Commerce Commission for 3 years and learned painfully that only my mother read my stories.

In this case, the journalist appeals to professional values despite her understanding that they seem to run contrary to a marketing perspective. Her paper's duty to serve as a "public record" takes precedence over her perception of readers' interest. (Note also how her years of "doing" news have shaped her understanding of audience interest.)

At other times, importance translates into giving voice to the voiceless. It is the motivating force for many journalists. For example, *Tribune* assistant metro editor Kerry Luft says that while he was in journalism school, he was having second thoughts about his profession until he was assigned a story while he was working for a Louisiana paper during a summer vacation:

> I did a piece about general assistance checks being cut in half. ... I found this old guy that lived in a room about this size [very small]. He had a bed in one corner and a chair that was rickety. He had an old black-and-white TV and all he got was $86 a month on general assistance; $75 of it went to rent this tiny little room, so he had $11 a month for everything else, and he didn't even have a phone. ... So, I wrote a story, and a week later I got a call from our bureau chief in Baton Rouge that said every desk in the legislature, that story was on it, and they voted that day and they restored the money.

This is a classic story of a journalist acting on behalf of the voiceless. The story is archetypal of the crusading journalist and is intrinsically bound to a professional values orientation. Luft continues:

> I went back to do a follow-up and found the guy and he said, "You know, you saved my life," and to this day when I think about that, I realize there is a force for good in journalism and it's those stories that are going to keep you going when you have to do the bank robberies, the messy divorce cases, the really slimy—there are days you come home and want to take a shower to scrub the slime off you, but you get those stories and it's worth it.

For *Tribune* metro editor Jean Davidson, importance can be translated into exposing wrongdoing. It becomes a vital part of her paper's overall mission:

> On a broader level, many stories I think of almost as a public service. Yesterday, we had a story about stowaway riders on the CTA [Chicago Transit Authority] who pop up after a crash and claim injury. I consider that story a public service ... the highlight of my day, incidentally, was when a personal injury lawyer called me, screaming, saying that [the story] had destroyed the image of personal injury lawyers. I got a good laugh out of that.

What is defined at these news organizations as important often does not fit a marketing orientation; at times it works quite to the contrary. It is a dilemma recognized among journalism scholars and practitioners. For example, Merrill (Dennis & Merrill, 1984) discussed his approach to the bind:

> A good editor is one who recognizes that it is a journalistic responsibility to provide the reader with some significant and useful news which may or not be of great immediate interest or appeal; at the same time, the editor knows that, in order to get the readers exposed to such news, he must also provide types of news of a more shallow—perhaps even sensational—nature. The good editor is a pragmatist and a realist, not some one-dimensional person seeking either to entertain or to educate. (p. 146)

The good editor, according to Merrill, will then work into his or her paper or newscast both interesting and important stories.

When the newspaper finds itself "obligated" to tell important stories that do not necessarily seem to make for a "good read," it will do the best it can to make the story interesting. For example, editors at the *Tribune* said they believed they needed to run an election story about some minor local contests in the winter of 1993. The problem was that they sensed little public interest in the contests. One of the paper's political editors put it this way:

> You knew we had to say something because here we were 3 days before an election—because you have an obligation to remind people "Hey, today's an election; get out to the polls," that sort of stuff. We had to do something, and we sat around saying nobody cares; well, let's do a story about nobody cares and why. So you wind up with a story that was interesting without the traditional parameters of the news.

The editors were caught in a bind between their professional values, which dictate that the election is "important," and a marketing orientation, which led them to believe that the story would be inherently boring to their audience. The key was to make the important story more interesting. So they had reporter Laurie Goering (1992) focus on good imaginative writing and peculiar details to make the story come alive:

> Democracy may be in the air in February, but there's a fierce wind-chill with it, and most voters just stay home. Plenty of others don't even know elections are going on. ...
>
> Pete Denhargog, superintendent of public works for south suburban Thornton, had to admit last week he had no idea an election for township supervisor, clerk, collector, highway commissioner and trustees was set for Tuesday.
>
> That's despite a campaign that has included the theft of more than 800 campaign signs, the arrest of a baseball-bat wielding political operative, $2,000 worth of scratched paint and punctured tires on campaign workers' cars and the untimely death of a trustee on incumbent Supervisor Frederick Redell's slate last week.
>
> Denhargog hadn't heard. Up since midnight plowing newly fallen snow, he stabbed a french fry on his plate at Cherie's Cafe in downtown Thornton and reflected as thoughtfully as anyone could after 24 hours without sleep.
>
> "No, I didn't know," he said. "Most people don't know. I saw a few signs."
>
> Will he vote now that he knows?
>
> "I vote when I feel like it," he said.
>
> How about this time?
>
> "Probably not." (p. 1)

In this case, professional values led the journalists to believe they had to say something about the upcoming election. So, they personalized the story by focusing on the views of a county worker at a diner to make the issue come alive and to provide a figure with whom their readers could identify.

The tie between journalism and government is deeply embedded in American journalism. The press has traditionally been labeled the "Fourth Estate." It is part of the rhetoric of most journalism texts, such as this message in Mencher's (1981) *News Reporting and Writing:*

> The journalist who is committed to the open society, to democratic values, has a moral structure from which to work. It seems clear that the journalist must be alert to institutions and their activities. ... Gans describes this in his "cluster" value system as "altruistic democracy." (p. 412)

Yet, although professional values dictate coverage of the election, a marketing orientation would lead the journalist to conclude that because people are not interested, the paper would do best not to cover the story at all. The compromise is to put the best spin on the story to generate interest.

Even when the news worker operates from a professional values perspective, the marketing orientation is seldom totally abandoned. For some such stories, the goal is to find a way to make the story interesting. Assistant metro editor Kerry Luft talks about putting together a story regarding the Governor's budget message:

> I don't think people are all that interested in what Jim Edgar's budget proposal is going to be today. I think they are more interested in how it shakes out down the line. It's important to do it [write the story], and the key is to try to make people care. If we can say tomorrow that property tax increases are on the horizon in Illinois because of this ... people care. You always have to try to find the reason why you care. ... The constant challenge is telling the readers why they should [care] too.

In this instance, the editor works to make peace between professional values of what he deems is important for his readers and a marketing orientation that elevates the news criterion of interest. He argues that the story is important, even as he admits that it is not inherently interesting. The resolution comes in his argument, "the key is to try to make people care." Luft argues that these "should tell" stories need to include a "Why do I care?" paragraph. Inherently, Luft is arguing that the good reporter can make the important story interesting by establishing a sense of personal impact for the news audience.

Tribune reporter William Recktenwald (1993) put the "Why do I care?" paragraph into a seemingly uninteresting story about setting up a testing schedule for police department promotions in Chicago (April 16, 1993):

> "Not having the number of detectives that you are budgeted for creates a work problem: It puts a greater strain and a heavier workload on the officers in place," Rodriguez said. "It's a reasonable assumption that not as many crimes are being solved. We have had to prioritize." (p. 1)

Notice that even Recktenwald's source, the police superintendent, has seemingly developed an understanding for showing personal impact in news stories. Without testing, there are fewer police promotions. Without police promotions, there are fewer detectives. With fewer detectives, there is more crime. With more crime, the audience is in more danger. Recktenwald uses the "Why do I care?" paragraph as a means for making an important story interesting. The "Why do I care?" paragraph resolves the tension between a marketing orientation that leads the journalist to "give 'em what they want" and a professional values orientation that says, "Give 'em what they need." The "Why do I care?" paragraph is an example of the journalist using personal *impact* to make the *important* story *interesting*.

IMPACT

Impact is another news value that is clearly tied to the news audience. It can function as the mediating value between a marketing orientation to the news and a professional values orientation. Yet, there is no one understanding about what connotes impact or whether it is always a good thing.

In his reporting text, *News Reporting and Writing,* Mencher (1981) listed impact as the first value in determining newsworthiness: "Impact: Events that are likely to affect many people. Here, journalists talk about significance, importance, the kinds of information that interest people or ... need to know to be informed" (p. 70). Notice that Mencher's definition of impact encompasses the two other news values discussed in this chapter, interest and importance.

Impact has a wide range of meanings for media scholars and for professional journalists and is therefore a "slippery" concept to explicate. It also goes by slightly different names with slightly different meanings. For example, Izard, Culbertson, and Lambert (1990) called it *consequence* and argued that the concept can be measured in terms of both the amount of impact an event has per person and on the number of persons affected by the news event. Carey (1986) argued that the journalist has succeeded when he can demonstrate *significance* for the audience.

Impact appears as a tantamount news value in both of the Chicago news rooms observed for this text. In recalling *The Chicago Tribune*'s coverage of the slaying of high school basketball star Ben Wilson, Carey (1986) argued that *significance* allowed the story to play for more days than it might have otherwise:

> At first, Ben Wilson became the personification of the problems of growing up Black. ... Wilson became a "news peg," a tragic death to be explained by the impersonal causes of poverty, unemployment, igno-rance, illiteracy, and hopelessness. ... Distinguished reporting of these conditions even had an effect. Gang violence was reported to be down 40 percent in the wake of Wilson's death and the coverage of it.

The coverage, however, also looked for the significance of the death of this young man. The significance was found in public forgetfulness a generation after the civil rights struggle and a half generation after the War on Poverty. ... *The Chicago Tribune* used the death of Ben Wilson to forcefully remind its readers of the meaning of life in urban America (pp. 193–194).

In 1992, the focus at the paper was on the slaying of a 9-year-old boy, Dantrell Davis, who was shot while holding his mother's hand as he walked to school one day. Editor Jean Davidson says *The Tribune* set up its "Killing Our Children" series to give greater exposure to the death of every child who had been violently killed in Chicago during the year. Davidson contends that the Davis story triggered the feature:

> We just made the decision that we were not going to let any kid die—and we made kind of a cut-off at [age] 14—without special notice and attention to the details of their lives. So, that carried us through

to the end of the year. We also made the commitment to look at some of the broad issues that caused this to happen. ... So, that was one event that was critical for all of us, that hence branched out into a real huge effort in reporting that I think pervades a lot of what we do here now. ... We were all just so struck by the fact that everything was in place that should have protected him, and yet, truly nobody could have protected him.

Perhaps the ultimate form of impact a reporter or news organization can hope for is that the reporting will actually prompt its audience to take action. The editor claims that such was the result of the paper's initial coverage of Dantrell Davis:

We got tremendous response from people who would call and say, "What can I do?" Even far removed from the violence. In suburban areas, schools. We developed a relationship with [the Edward] Jenner School where he went to school and other inner-city schools. I think that it had a very profound effect on many, many people ... . [We received] a lot of phone calls, a lot of letters. Tremendous feedback. I don't ever recall feedback like that on another story.

The news organization deemed this sort of feedback as evidence that the series was having some real impact on its audience. This is a stronger claim than simply one of significance, as Carey argued was the case of Ben Wilson. This coverage was having a real impact on readers' emotions and in their responses to the story. This is where the notion of "impact" fits into the news equation. Journalists' professional values tell them that the slaying of a 7-year-old boy on his way to school is important, but it is also heart-rending and frightening. Indeed, it transcends these two characteristics to become the quintessential story with "impact." The staff hopes its overall effort will make a real change in people's lives and, in turn, help reduce the homicide rate, just as the paper claimed following the Ben Wilson incident. Reporter Bill Recktenwald keeps track of these kinds of statistics:

I think we'll make a difference by the end of the year. I hope. Right this week we were over 14 [youth violently killed] yesterday. I think we can make a difference because if we tell people, "you know, you pick up your kid, you just lose it, and you get so angry, and you just shake that kid, you're liable to kill it," that can make a difference; it doesn't take that many people saying, "Oh, maybe I shouldn't do that," and there are other things too.

One *Tribune* story in which a reporter was able to show how an important event has direct impact on his readers' pocketbooks was Recktenwald's (1992) front-page story, "One Man Suffers, We All Pay." The story began this way:

> Darnell McGee was the 8,044th shooting victim in Chicago this year, the bloodiest and most violent year in the city's history. He was an accidental target on a warm summer's evening in a nice neighborhood.
>
> His case didn't produce a line in the newspaper, a blurb on TV. There were no community meetings, no expressions of outrage like those that followed the death of 7-year-old Dantrell Davis, shot by a sniper on his way to school in the Cabrini-Green housing development.
>
> McGee, a personable 17-year-old high school student, was critically injured but lived. His case was just a statistical blip in the mind-boggling 12,948 shootings in the city in the first 10 months of the year, about one every 34 minutes.
>
> Yet, it is estimated that a single case such as McGee's could end up costing society at least $1 million in medical expenses alone and perhaps a half million or more in police, court, and prison costs. (p. 1)

In this story, crime, which is often merely *interesting,* also becomes *important*—a social issue—in a way that has real impact on the reader. In reviewing the story, Recktenwald suggests that this story would play even to readers in suburban Shaumburg, far away from the danger of urban Chicago:

> Most people don't realize the cost. If you live in Shaumburg, you think that's happening to those people down there, and the fact is that the bills are being paid by the people up there. And it [the story] got incredible amounts of good comments from colleagues, letters from people in the mail, [who] found it was an interesting way to tell a story that hadn't been told.

Once again, the *important* story has been told in an *interesting* way. The tie between the professional orientation of the journalist and the marketing orientation is the news value *impact*. The journalist was able to show how an important, but otherwise less interesting story, had an impact even on suburban readers. They are paying for the urban crime.

Sometimes, the impact is less direct; in fact it is hypothetical. The journalist attempts to make the case that the story he or she tells about someone else could also someday effect the reader or that the story being told is not unique—that it applies to a good many people.

WGN reporter Roseann Tellez suggests that it is that hypothetical impact that made her station's coverage of a suburban Chicago couple who left their children alone for several days better than it might have been otherwise:

> But it really showed that these kids—the safety of kids is being jeopardized every day in all different types of neighborhoods. We did expand the story to talk about the problem of people leaving their children home alone even on the South side or wherever for these other problems. So, we took a look at the bigger problem.

Impact is not always a positive attribute in news stories. Sometimes news workers are concerned that a story might have adverse impact on their audience, that is, that the story will be a turn-off for viewers. For example, WGN executive producer Tony Noce contends that that is an especially pertinent concern in crime stories:

> You always have that kind of limit. How much is that going to impact a person? Will it impact them so much because you're showing too much of a graphic crime scene that [you] will turn them off and not focus in on what crime is really doing to the city? And if you don't show enough, then it becomes too blasé to impact them.

Noce says such a fear leads his station to look for a happy medium in its coverage. He says, for example, that his station will only show a picture of a corpse on rare occasions, depending on the crime. He says that the station is more likely to show police carrying a body bag than to show a close-up of a corpse.

Sometimes, perceived negative impact on audience members can also cause editors to kill a story. WGN Producer Tim Jackson says fear of panicking his audience caused him to not air a story about a west-coast fast-food chain in which 50 cases of food poisoning were reported:

> The problem appears to be under-cooked beef. I thought that was interesting because lots of us eat in fast-food chains one time or another during the course of our eating habits in the week. Do we care about that? Yeah. Is it alarming? Yes. Is it going to scare the living daylights out of the people that we're talking to? Maybe.

Jackson says he spent 10 minutes discussing the merits of the story with his writer before opting to kill the story:

What we decided collectively was we're not going to run it. ... We [felt] that we were going to ... scare the living daylights out of the public about all fast-food chains, because that's what TV does. ... People immediately call up and they say, "So, are all fast-food hamburgers bad?" That's what they say. We didn't say that, but that is what the viewer deduces from what we say. They call up and go, "All blood is bad, right? All blood has AIDS in it. Isn't that right?" ...I can almost quote you.

Hypothetically, negative impact on viewers killed the story. Based on past experience constructing similar stories, the editor has formed a tacit understanding of his audience. He has been led to believe that a good portion of his audience is prone to be alarmists.

Still, more often than not, when news workers talk about impact, the concept is positive. They hope their coverage will affect their audience in a positive way. One type of impact reporters hope to achieve in their stories is that the information presented becomes useful for their audience. In one story, WGN reporter Roseann Tellez hoped to do just that:

One story I did [was] about a job-search hotline that was being conducted. So, naturally you want to put yourself in the shoes of people who are looking for jobs and you want to think, "What are the things most important to them about finding a job at this time period?" And so you would ask, well, really it's basic to any type of story, "What are people going to be most interested in?" But in this case, especially, I tried to put myself in the shoes of someone who is unemployed and offer them information I thought would be helpful.

Tellez included a number of direct suggestions to her audience for those looking for work. Her story was likely gratifying for her because she felt she was really able to connect with her viewers in a very tangible way and offer advice that a portion of them could immediately use. This story had immediate application for some viewers and an application that most could use at some point in their careers. Tellez attempted to make the story as interesting as possible by making it as relevant and useful to the unemployed person as possible. In other stories, the impact is not so direct. Sometimes, the impact is indirect, in that viewers can learn something by watching problems encountered in other geographic areas. Tellez recounts another WGN story:

There was a story we did on the proposed nuclear waste dump site in Martinsville. And, even though that was something that was kind of on the fringe of our coverage area, we thought it was of great importance because it's determining how Illinois is going to deal with its nuclear waste. And we had a time limit on it, which we have since blown off and nothing's happened, but we're supposed to have some kind of a waste site in place by a certain date. So it's something that even though Martinsville was the site being investigated at the time, it's the kind of thing that could wind up in anybody's neighborhood.

In this case, the notion of impact is very much akin to the reporter's definition of importance. The Martinsville story becomes of interest to the viewer when the reporter makes the case that this danger "could wind up in anybody's neighborhood." She establishes personal relevance or impact for her viewers. Again, the important story has been made interesting. Impact, in this sense, is some change in the viewers' understanding of their world so that they will be readied to take action if need be.

In some situations, the reporter's goal is to make the news come alive for the audience. Reporters want to make an impact on the viewers because they deem it important. WGN executive producer Tony Noce suggests that personal impact is his goal for his station's depiction of crime stories, "I'd like it to bring home that this stuff is really happening. This is not a movie where the people after they get shot get up and walk away. [I'd like to make] an impact to try to do something about it." Impact in this case translates into personal involvement. By making the news "real," the journalist again succeeds in making what he or she deems "important" interesting, or at least engaging.

The goal is to make the important story interesting. Impact is the tool by which the journalist hopes to accomplish his or her goal. Personal impact leads the audience to take an interest in that which the journalist deems important. WGN assistant news director Jim Disch argues that that becomes a reward for the journalist:

I think, at a very basic level, people who like this business—they like it because they know it has an impact on viewers; you know, you can connect. I think, we think about impact a lot. If you're doing a new medical story, you know that impacts the audience. ... We can do investigative pieces that will drive people out of business. When an investigation starts, a legal investigation, because of something that you've done, you know there is impact there. When you do the medical stories, you mention a victim's name, and money starts rolling in.

We're not in the fund-raising business, but we know that there is an impact there also.

Disch has used the term *impact* in a variety of ways. When he first talks about "doing a medical story," he is referring to having an impact as being personally relevant to the viewer. When he is talking about "driving people out of business," he treats impact as making the viewer's world a bit better. When he talks about raising money for a victim, he treats impact as something that compels the viewer to take action.

Impact, as presented in this section, ranges greatly in meaning, much as did notions of interest. When journalists use the term *impact,* they have not necessarily sorted out all of those meanings for themselves. Viewing the body of a corpse has quite a different impact from showing a reader how his or her taxes may go up. Impact may be translated as providing the audience with personally relevant information. Fear of negative impact may cause journalists to kill certain stories or reshape others. When impact is viewed in these ways, it fits with a marketing perspective.

Impact may also mean forcing audience members to face up to societal problems and grapple with solutions. It may mean forcing self-examination. It may mean providing information so that audience members can help make their environment safer. It may mean righting wrongs. When impact is viewed in these ways, it fits more closely with a professional values perspective.

Overall, impact functions as a mediating value of newsworthiness between interest and importance. By demonstrating personal impact with their audience, the journalist is able to make an important story interesting. The audience member takes interest in the stories the journalists feel they ought to tell.

CONCLUSION

When asked which news values are the most important, *Tribune* transportation writer Gary Washburn offers a typical response:

> Certainly, impact of what you're talking about—how widespread it is, how far-reaching, how many people it affects... that's certainly a big factor, as is the interest value. Off the top of my head, I guess those are two big ones. Some stories you need to do because they're important, although they may not be interesting. They're oatmeal type stories; they don't taste particularly good going down, but they're good for you. And then obviously there are some stories that are interesting,

but they're light ... there might not be a lot to them, but the good story is the one that both has impact on people and is a good read.

Washburn's response shows how notions of interest and importance blur into the news value of impact for journalists. Impact becomes a synthesis of the other two news values.

Reporters, editors, and producers in these news organizations all recognize the need to interest their audiences. Print journalists know that they are competing with TV and a host of other factors in the lives of their audience members. TV reporters know that their effectiveness in interesting their audience will be reflected in ratings. Anchors know that Q-scores will help determine their salaries at contract time. They want to resolve the inherent tensions between their professional values, which suggest that they write about what is important, and a marketing orientation, which leads them to focus on what is considered interesting. That resolution can come when the journalist is able to show impact.

As a news value, impact can be the hardest to explicate because it takes on such a variety of meanings for these journalists. Yet, it tends to take on greater meaning than the other news values when it is used to resolve the tension between the professional and marketing orientations. The news value has an almost synergistic quality when it is used to tie interest to importance.

Yet, which definitions of impact or of newsworthiness are ultimately highlighted will vary depending on which person in the news organization one approaches. Those predominantly concerned with garnering higher ratings figures or greater circulation figures will see the job, their audience, and news values in one perspective. Those who are predominantly focused on cranking out news stories by deadlines will see them quite differently. In chapter 5, I address those varying perspectives.

Chapter 5

The Audience From Different Organizational Levels

"Let us go to the palace," said one blind man. ... A friend of the six blind men met them at the palace and an elephant was standing in the courtyard. The six blind men touched the elephant with their hands.

... "An elephant is like a wall," said the first blind man. "A wall?" said the second blind man. "You're wrong," said the second blind man. "An elephant is like a snake." The third blind man said, "You're wrong. An elephant is like a spear." The fourth blind man said, "No, you're wrong. An elephant is like a tree." ...

The Rajah looked out and saw the blind men arguing in the courtyard. "Stop," called the Rajah. "The elephant is a big animal. Each man touched only one part. You must put all the parts together to find out what an elephant is like." (From *The Blind Men and the Elephant,* as retold by Lillian Quigley, 1959.)

Just as the blind men all derived different images of what constituted an elephant based on their limited access to the animal, one can develop very different images of the news audience depending on whom one talks to within journalistic organizations. Audience imagery is real among journalists and is a powerful input in constructing the news, but it is not uniform. Although, as was demonstrated earlier, much is tacit and embedded within the routines and values of news gathering, some audience imagery is also explicit. It is made real through a variety of tools (research) and experiences (phone calls, letters-to-the-editor, discussions). Differing views of the audience are dependent on which level of analysis one chooses to highlight. Whitney and Ettema (1991) argued for examining new levels of analysis in media-audience studies: "Images or models of the audience need not reside only in the heads of individuals; they may reside in the goals and practices of institutions" (p. 9). Similarly, Hirsch (1977) argued that concepts (such as images of the audience) are best understood when considered on differing levels of analysis, "with each helping the others [levels] present alternative interpretations of findings or raise new questions for investigation" (p. 18).

Even journalism practitioners recognize the need to consider their audiences from different perspectives. For example, Kennedy, Moen and Ranly (1993) at the University of Missouri School of Journalism have encouraged writers to consult individuals and departments throughout their publication's organization to learn more about the audience for whom they are writing.

Within news organizations, individuals have different functional goals and subsequently develop different images of who or what constitutes their audiences. I argue in this book that one can grasp a better understanding of the organizational approaches to audience by examining the views of audience at different vocational levels within those organizations. In this chapter, I examine notions of the news audience at three different levels within the news organizations: reporters and news gatherers; editors and producers; and senior editors, producers, and news directors. In addition, I examine the key job goals at each level, because such goals help shape the outlook by which audience is understood.

In this chapter, I also address the ways in which news employees form impressions of their audiences based on direct contact with audience members, with knowledge garnered from formal studies of the audience, and from tacit understandings developed while engaged in news work. In addition, such understandings can be categorized according to how they first come to the news workers' attention. Some understandings about the news audience develop out of audience members' reactions to a particular story (*content-mediated* information), and other understandings about the audience are based on research on the audience conducted by news workers or their organizations (*research-mediated* information).

REPORTERS AND NEWS GATHERERS

Reporters and news gatherers, by and large, see their primary goal as producing the news product: stories and visuals. Therefore, their impression of the audience is, perhaps, the least tangible and is more tacit. Audience imagery stems from their work and from the news product. For example, the focus of a stringer photographer at WGN-TV is on selling his wares to WGN and other stations. Reporter Steve Sanders asks stringer David Weaver about his work:

> **Sanders**: Tell me, you turn out a good piece of work and five TV stations buy it in Chicago, which is not unusual, and that's 150 bucks a piece?
> **Weaver**: Right.
> **Sanders**: That's $750 a day for one story.
> **Weaver**: Well, you gotta realize, yeah, that's one story. Most are not going to be "five-station" sales, especially because [Channels] 5 [NBC] and 32 [Fox] buy hardly anything.
> **Sanders**: They don't?
> **Weaver**: No, their budgets are shot. Two [CBS] buys a lot, 9 [WGN] buys a lot, 7 [ABC] buys a moderate amount. So, most of them if they're big are gonna be like "three-station" sales. You've got to have something really exclusive and really good to have "five-station" sales. Because with so many stringers now, like sometimes two stringers will get these stations and the other stringer will get three stations. Unless one stringer gets there really quick and gets something really live.

The stringer is not especially concerned about his audience, but instead his goal is to sell as many stories to as many stations as he can. Still, his conversation reflects some understanding of what stations deem as important for their viewers: live or breaking stories or stories that are exclusive. The connection is perhaps clearer when the rhetoric of a general assignment reporter is examined. After WGN reporter Mary Gannon finishes a discussion she just had with her assignment editor over whether to cover a story involving a fatal car accident, she offers her impression of the news value of such stories. When probed, her rhetoric reflects a conception of her audience:

> Traffic accidents are of no interest to people. That's my opinion. To me it's "small town" and we've got a lot bigger things going on in Chicago. We don't need to cover traffic accidents, unless there's something unique about it.

As I argued in previous chapters, tacit understandings of her audience help shape the reporter's view of the product. Although she is principally concerned with generating stories, an understanding of what interests her audience is imbedded in the process. Undoubtedly, her view of her audience also reinforces her own preferences for avoiding such coverage. On the other hand, her preferences for avoiding such coverage likely reinforces her perception that her audience is not interested in those stories.

Tribune reporter Steve Johnson says that audience comes to mind when he is writing about highly charged issues in which there are clear sides that oppose each other. Johnson says such a situation will cause him to pay closer attention to accuracy: "Maybe I'll read back through [my story] three times instead of two times and double-check my facts three times instead of two times." *Tribune* transportation writer Gary Washburn says he sometimes writes for transportation professionals, a classic example of a *reference group* audience image:

> I guess sometimes when I write, I want to make it weighty enough so that a person who is in the profession—a transit professional, some-body in the airlines or whatever—can appreciate the import of it and ... the sophistication of it. So, I guess in the back of my mind that kind of person might exist, certainly also the person who drops 50 cents into the [newspaper vending] machine is somebody who I try to keep in mind ... so that man or that woman can come away after plunking that 50 cents into the machine and read the story and get something out [of it].

Although audience image is tacitly involved in story construction, not all knowledge of audience among reporters and news gatherers is tacit—reporters can and do talk about what they learn from audience contacts. Some knowledge is based on direct encounters with the audience, phone calls, talk on the street, and observation. Other knowledge about the audience is obtained from formal audience studies.

Tribune reporter Bill Recktenwald says his stories periodically prompt phone calls from his readers. For example, after running a year-end story on all the youth who were killed in Chicago-area gangs in 1992, Recktenwald said he heard from his readers:

> I got calls that Sunday down here saying, "You ruined my whole Sunday." Good. That's actually what I was hoping to do. We wanted to jar people, to slap people upside the head and say, "Hey, this is very serious. Kids can't walk down the street in nice neighborhoods and in poor neighborhoods." ... It jarred a lot of public officials into action.

In another instance, after writing the story of a young Chicago Bulls fan who was shot, Recktenwald said three readers called in offering the youth tickets to a Bulls game. WGN reporter Roseann Tellez says she has contact with audience members as she works. She says she has heard a great deal of response to a new Saturday morning news show she anchors: "I can't tell you how many people have come up and said, 'I'm always out on Friday night' or 'I never stay up late and it's great to tune in in the morning and see what's going on.'"

Like Tellez, most of the understandings among reporters and news gatherers about their audiences is developed out of work with those stories or newscasts; that is, it is content-mediated information about the news audience. Audience image develops from audience reaction to news stories and from the journalist's work in building those stories. Recktenwald believes he has truly connected with his readers when one calls in to say Recktenwald "ruined his whole day." But although much of the direct contact with audience members is content-mediated, flowing out of work with specific stories, not all of it is. Some stories flow out of direct observations of the audience. Some understandings are developed by a reporter's informal observations of audience members. Tellez says she often judges what is interesting to people by what she personally hears discussed: "We all kind of know what everybody is talking about out there. ... It might be because just the day before I was sitting somewhere and everybody was talking about a particular problem in the city or something."

Beyond direct contact with individuals, reporters have differing views and differing levels of awareness of formal analyses of the audience. Tellez, for example, says ratings mean little to her. Anchor and reporter Steve Sanders is aware that the midday news, which he anchors, has an older demographic, as do most midday news shows. However, he reports only a secondhand knowledge of the audience figures for the station's evening newscast:

> I can tell you what I've been told about the primary audience and that would be at 9 o'clock—a slightly older group of individuals that is relatively more affluent than the [average] viewer in Chicago, and that is because these are individuals with long hours—go to work early in the morning and come home late at night. And it's often the case that they go to bed early. The one late newscast they want to turn to is the 9 o'clock news.

At the *Tribune,* transportation reporter Gary Washburn says he doesn't see the formal analyses:

> Not only don't I make use of them, but those things are really not made available to staff. I mean something might dribble out here or there in a company publication ... where we get some information about a survey, but they're not generally circulated.

Workers at lower occupational levels within news organizations receive a greater proportion of their understandings about the audience from content-mediated sources than from research-mediated sources. Still, most reporters do seem to possess a general awareness of formal research-mediated audience information, some more so than others. For example, *Tribune* general assignment reporter Steve Johnson can recite the circulation figures for each of the paper's five zones. Johnson says he came to learn the data when he became frustrated that his stories were not carried in all zones, "Then I saw the north/south zoning figures [in which his story was carried] are a lot bigger than all the other zones. So, it makes you feel less bad about being zoned out of the suburbs."

Johnson says he also pays attention to marketing studies conducted at the paper, but he is skeptical about the results:

> The marketing department is always commissioning studies about who reads what section of the paper and what people want to see more of in the paper, and frankly, I just don't believe them because in one of the studies, people said they don't want to see more news about celebrities and I mean, come on. This is just a case of someone telling an interviewer what he or she thinks they want to hear. So I tend to disbelieve a lot of that stuff.

By and large, reporters and news gatherers form impressions about their audiences stemming from tacit understandings that grow out of their on-the-job experience and from direct contact with sources and audience members and from their superiors (editors, news directors, etc.). Most of this information is content-mediated, stemming from reactions to particular stories. To a lesser degree, reporters learn about their audiences from direct observation of audience members and from information that trickles down from organizational studies and analyses—research-mediated information.

EDITORS AND PRODUCERS

Editors and producers' views of the audience typically stem from a bit wider variety of sources and experiences. Although reporters and news gatherers see their key task as producing stories, editors and producers are more concerned with the overall news product: the television show or the daily paper. For example, WGN producer Tim Jackson felt good about the news show he had just produced:

I'm proud of the show. ... It presents many challenges because we're very fast-paced. We're almost completely computer-driven. And because of the size of our operation, which is very lean, to pull off what we pulled off [a newscast with several live and breaking stories] was borderline miracle.

Although these middle-level workers are more concerned with the overall news product, they are also concerned with the individual pieces that make up the newscast or newspaper. For example, *Tribune* metro editor Jean Davidson says she wants to be as ambitious for every story as possible: "I really want to see hard-hitting broad stories in a daily paper. Not just for a Sunday magazine kind of paper. I'm also looking for the impact on community and I am very concerned with writing quality." The editor's broader focus on her product expands her view of her audience and the kind of impact she would like her paper to have on the community. She talks about different kinds of impact on the community. For example, she suggests that, at times, she can judge a story's emotional impact on her audience based on her own emotional reaction.

Like reporters and news gatherers, editors and producers base their assessments of the audience on personal interactions with audience members and their reactions to stories (content-mediated information), as well as from the results of formal audience studies (research-mediated information.) *Tribune* photo assignment editor Frank Hames says he learned about his audience from the radio after the *Tribune* featured a photo spread that depicted a 16-year-old gunshot victim who died on a hospital gurney:

I was listening to the talk shows on the radio and there were people calling in on both sides saying, "Well, the photographs should have been used and [they] should not have been used," but ... once people seemed to understand that we were trying to make a point ... a lot of them seemed to understand....

The learning experience for Hames was a clear example of content-mediated audience information; it grew out of readers' reactions to a specific photo spread. Yet, Hames also indicates that he learns about his audience from personal contact. These interactions can occasionally focus on stories that have run in the paper (content-mediated audience information), but they can also offer Hames a more general understanding of his audience (what might be termed *relationship-mediated* information):

You meet people on the street. I belong to a couple [of] different organizations, and I have a lot of friends and I'm pretty active in my neighborhood and community stuff like that. ... You meet people outside the news business and you see them once a week ... and they'll ask you, "Hey, what do you hear on this? ... Have you heard anything?"

Those personal contacts do shape the news worker's concept about what his or her audience is like, that is, about their tastes and standards of what should or should not be in the daily paper. Phone calls play a particularly significant role in shaping these news workers' understandings of their audience. For example, WGN writer and producer Tim Jackson says his station distributes a call sheet to its news workers each morning that logs the subject matter of each call coming into the station's switchboard. Jackson says the sheet is brought to the staff's attention each morning by news director Paul Davis:

This morning ... he came out and said, "Well, I see we got four calls for the usage of the word *decapitated* describing one of the victims who died in the train tragedy yesterday." That came across to a handful of viewers as very offensive. We paid attention to it. I don't believe we said that word again.

Jackson says he now takes more notice of phone calls than he did a few years earlier in his career:

My first 5 years of being in the business I would have argued with that and said the viewer is stupid or that caller must be out of his mind. Well, that doesn't really matter. ... We have access to information and privileges that other people don't have, but we're "worker bees." And if we ever forget that, I think that we're forgetting who we're serving. And if somebody calls up who is our viewer and says, "I don't like it when you use the word *decapitated*. It upset my child and it upset my elderly mother. I was having my tomato soup." If there's another way that we can say that, ... so then we make a note of it.

Jackson's years of working with the news have altered his view about his job and his audience. He now sees it as imperative to take his audience's views more seriously. Phone calls are also taken seriously at *The Chicago Tribune*. Metro editor Jean Davidson fields many calls herself:

I'm one of the first editors here in the morning. There's really not much of a mechanism to screen calls. Anybody who calls the *Tribune* in the morning, it seems like, talks to me. So, I get a lot of nuts and I get a lot of people who are angry because we transposed the lottery numbers. And I get those people too, who I really like to hear from. I mean, it gives me a base I guess. ... It helps to get feedback from the people you are writing for so it doesn't seem like you just talk ... in a vacuum.

The phone calls help the editor "form a base." Davidson says she especially likes to hear from "ordinary readers," particularly those from "far-flung communities ... people who have their ear to the ground." Phone calls make audience feedback a real input into the news construction process. The information stemming from phone calls is typically content-mediated audience information. Understandings about audience are formed from listening to and reading direct audience reactions to the news stories aired or printed.

Editors also form impressions about their audiences from direct observation. The *Tribune*'s political editor Kerry Luft plays detective when he is on the train and monitors which passengers are reading the *Tribune* and which are reading the rival *Sun Times*. The editor develops an understanding of his audience by simple observation. Yet, Luft, like a portion of other producers and editors, seems to take a fascination with formalized audience data. For example, he said that for a period of time he obtained information from the circulation desk on each time a subscriber canceled the paper due to his or her disfavor with the paper's political coverage. He has also monitored the ways in which his paper has expanded its circulation:

The traditional *Tribune* readership has always been a White, suburban, upper middle-class paper—always has been. Then watch, how did we expand? DuPage County—which is White, suburban middle class. Northwest suburbs, Lake County—White suburban, very upper middle class. It's only now that we stretch out other ways. If we felt that our base was working people, we could concentrate a lot more on the city than we do.

At WGN, noon producer Forrest Respess also has a keen notion for the constitution of his noontime audience. He is proud of his newscast's audience and bases his assessment on both formal ratings and more casual observations:

We're the highest independent rated midday newscast in the country. Last year we were the 11th highest of all midday newscasts in the country. And as far as WGN is concerned, we have the largest share of any program on this station. The closest thing to us is *Geraldo*, who precedes us, and he very seldom comes any closer than five share points to us. ... Our demographics show that a large part of our audience is older. One of our younger people came in, who lives in the uptown area, and he was saying ... if he's walking down where he lives, every bar, every place where you go by, they're tuned to our news.

So Respess concludes that there is a big portion of his noontime audience that is not recorded by ratings services because ratings only reflect at-home viewing. The bulk of his knowledge about his audience seems to be research-mediated information from formalized research, but some, stemming from casual observations by a news worker, may again be akin to "relationship-mediated" information. Still, although much of Respess' understanding of audience stems from observation and formal analyses, he, like other editors and producers, intuits much understanding about his audience based on his work. This information is largely content-mediated audience information. Respess, again, conveys a tacit knowledge of his audience:

I'm a strong believer in just instinct. ... There is just something—you look at a story, you look at a piece of talent and you know whether you like it or don't.... You have a feeling if it's good or not. ... [It comes from] inside—and maybe years of experience in the business.

In this case, Respess' knowledge of his audience is based on tacit knowledge that grows out of his work on individual stories and newscasts. It is another example of what Schön referred to as knowing-in-action. The "knowing" is not clearly verbalized, but comes from a storehouse of knowledge developed over time. As Schön expressed:

In some cases, we were once aware of the understandings that were subsequently internalized in our feeling for the stuff of action. In other cases, we may never have been aware of them. In both cases, however, we are usually unable to describe the knowing which our action reveals. (p. 54)

For WGN assignment editor Mike Kertez, the key to action seems to be in forming an implicit identification with his audience, using himself as a prototypical audience member:

Frankly, though, you don't have to teach what news is. Everybody knows what news is. If it's something you're going to tell your wife about ... that's what makes it newsworthy. ... There is really no way to define it. What makes it news is what makes it interesting. If it's not interesting, it's not going to be news to anybody.

Both Respess and Kertez use themselves as what Gans (1979) labeled "audience representative." They view the audience as being very much like themselves. They assume that their station's viewers have the same curiosities and the concerns as they do. Within the process of constructing news, they have constructed an image of the audience, on which they further construct the news. In general, editors and producers form images of their audiences tacitly from their work and more consciously from audience members who respond to their news product and from formal research.

SENIOR EDITORS, PRODUCERS, AND NEWS DIRECTORS

At the highest levels in the newsrooms, senior editors, producers, and news directors appear to voice the most sophisticated understandings of their audiences, stemming from both philosophical understandings of what they are working to accomplish and from formalized research-mediated information about their audience. That may well be because they are also forced to maintain a keen understanding of the function of news for information companies: to earn profits. WGN assistant news director Jim Disch points to that emphasis:

As a manager, I think over the years there has been ... just the common goal of knowing, "Yes, we have to inform people, but it has to be in the context of increasing ratings and making money with some of this stuff." We don't stay on the air at 12 noon and 9 o'clock if we're losing a few million bucks a year pumping the product out. Back here [the news director] and myself, the [executive producer], whoever, we know it's our job ultimately to make money for the company.

At *The Chicago Tribune,* managing editor Dick Ciccone admits that his organization's focus on profitability is alarming to his reporters:

> We're far more market-driven [today] and the '80s were a very bad period for the newspapers because they looked like they were [just] licenses to print money, and now in the '90s, it's very threatening because you have people like Charley [Brumback, chairman of the board of the Tribune Company] going in *Forbes* magazine saying we have to get out of the business of putting ink on paper. That's very debilitating for a staff of reporters here who hear the chairman of your company saying we have to get out of that business.

These editors and news directors are, of course, keenly aware of their organizations' goals of making profits. That view also helps shape their understanding of their product, which in turn, shapes their view of the audience. For example, at the *Tribune,* profits are maximized when the paper is zoned, with different information appealing to different audiences. Editor Ciccone contends that since the paper sells better in the north and northwest regions of Chicago, information is tailor-made for those sections. An understanding that the paper's ultimate goal is earning a profit leads to a product designed to appeal to audiences understood to be highly segmented.

The WGN-TV news department's emphasis on earning profits compels it to conduct independent audience research every 2 to 3 years. In addition, senior producers and news directors are keenly aware of both overnight and monthly ratings. To the lay person, the rhetoric used can sound like a foreign language. Assistant news director Jim Disch discusses recent trends at the station:

> I see we got a 1.8 on the weekend morning news, a 2.0 on the other, it's been playing like that for weeks, no great surprise. The 9 o'clock show on Sunday night did a 10.9. That's dynamite—double figures for an independent. Match three quarter-hours and then we had "Instant Replay," but we sustained at 10.9 for three quarter-hours—that's coming out of a 6.1 lead-in, actually a 5.5, 'cause we started climbing that last quarter-hour we went on the air. So that's quite a jump.

In this view, the audience is understood as a number. In this rhetoric, the producer only speaks of the size of his audience, not of any qualitative dimensions. Yet, those numbers are implicitly used to judge the quality of that which is produced. Disch says the numbers can be used to determine if special features are having an impact on ratings:

> These things are interesting to look at if you were promoting the heck out of a story or plugging a story into a movie and doing the movie

tie-in—kind of look and see if there is any indication that you helped spark the ratings.

This greater reliance on formalized research-mediated under-standings of their audience suits these senior editors, producers, and news directors well, given their task according to Ang (1991):

> Industry people need a kind of knowledge that allows them to act, not paralyze them—a convenient kind of knowledge that enables the industry to concoct its relation to the audience in a simple, clear-cut, and manageable way. Ratings discourse offers this knowledge because it puts together a streamlined map of "television audience." (p. 63)

Although ratings analyses are clearly recognized as important at the senior levels of the newsroom, there is also an effort to encourage the rest of the staff to consider the data as well, according to WGN's assistant news director, Jim Disch:

> Paul [the news director] and I have routinely looked at ratings and then put them out on the assignment desk for anyone to look at in the news department. Many years ago that was secret stuff. We think it's healthy for people to see ratings and in terms of how we're doing and if there is a good show. … It is important for the person to see "Oh my God, there were 3,000 households watching my show last night. That was just in the Chicago area."

Beyond the ratings information, the station conducts independent audience research that probes audience members on a number of factors related to the news, including their positive or negative reactions to anchorpersons and their interest in different kinds of stories. Executive producer Tony Noce says those results offer quali-tative information about the news audience:

> You get some idea, what is the age of your audience—How old? So, you can gauge the kind of stories—some of the interests of your audience in that age group. Do they want more health stories? More financial stories?

Audience research helps the news organization determine what kind of news appeals to audience interests. Although *The Chicago Tribune* also conducts formalized audience research, senior journal-ists there, like managing editor Dick Ciccone, often voice skepticism about their results:

> We have readership studies to see what readers lie about. We don't do much focus [group] studies on news. Readership is always the same. Ninety percent say they read the front page, which means 90% see the front page. Thirty-eight to 40% say they read the editorial page because that's what they are supposed to answer the pollsters.

That jaded view of the research is typical for journalists, according to Gans (1979). He suggested four reasons for their skepticism of audience research:

1. Journalists typically come from liberal arts backgrounds and dislike statistics.
2. Journalists have not been shown that such information is useful.
3. Audience research may cast "doubt on their news judgment and their professional autonomy" (p. 232).
4. Audience research is typically under the auspices of nonjournalists.

The skeptical views of the top editors at the *Tribune* also appear to translate into the way readership findings are disseminated throughout the organization. For example, even metro editor Jean Davidson reports that she generally does not receive readership study results and only hears about them anecdotally.

Yet, although general audience information from formalized research is at times treated with skepticism, content-mediated audience information, particularly from phone calls, plays an important role in creating an awareness of the audience, even at these highest levels of the *Tribune* newsroom. Managing editor Ciccone says phone calls can shape what the newspaper does. He says, for example, if the paper receives 10 to 12 complaints about some small change it has made, the paper will likely undo the change. He says such a reaction is "an awful lot of people to call this newspaper." Phone calls make a difference at the highest levels of the WGN newsroom as well. News director Paul Davis reviews the telephone logs daily to gauge audience reaction to his newscasts.

In these instances, however, news managers are most likely to make stylistic changes rather than substantive changes. For example, a number of complaints called into WGN-TV caused Davis to suggest that the word decapitated not be used in a report. Similarly, a number of phone calls to The Chicago Tribune newsroom persuaded Ciccone to call for changes in a new graphic presented in the paper.

Generally, one finds the most complex conceptions of audience expressed at the higher levels of the news operations. It tends to be a view based on several inputs rather than on just one or two. For example, WGN assistant news director Jim Disch argues that a number of elements are used to assess the strengths or weaknesses of anchor persons in attracting or appealing to an audience:

> The research helps a lot, and it's a mix between research, feedback you get from viewers through the phone calls, and letters,—especially when people are not liking certain people ... and sure, you go by your personal cluster, and the person's performance on the air, and your gut....

Last, at this level in the organization, senior editors, producers, and news directors appear to have developed broader philosophical notions of their news operation's functions and its relation to its audience. Their talk is illustrative of Schön's extension of knowing-in-action to *reflecting-in-action*. At times, the professional steps back from the work process and contemplates what is being done. It is at those moments that the professional is able to voice philosophical understandings about the work accomplished and the audience being served. Those philosophical views stemming from such reflecting-in-action are important in, for example, selecting news stories. *Tribune* managing editor Dick Ciccone argues that the audience should not direct coverage:

> Subscribers don't want a role in choosing what they get in the newspaper. That's why they buy the newspaper. They want me to tell them [that] the most important thing that happened in the world yesterday was the U.S. is trying to shore up Yeltsin's regime. They want me to tell them that.

Similarly, WGN news director Paul Davis has formed a philosophical view of what he hopes his station is doing for its audience: "I think we would like to think people learn something—that we may not give them many nuggets of pure truth, but we give them things that help them test their own attitudes and moods about things."

Overall, senior editors, producers, and news directors tend to have a more sophisticated understanding of their audiences based on a number of factors: tacit knowledge stemming from their day-to-day work in overseeing the news operation, direct response from audi-

ence members, formalized research, and philosophical understandings about what they feel they are trying to accomplish. They
also have the clearest understandings of the relation of the news to
broader organizational goals that are geared toward earning profits.

AN EXAMPLE OF CONTRASTING
ORGANIZATIONAL VIEWS OF AN
AUDIENCE

In 1992, Chicago's CBS-owned-and-operated station, WBBM, Channel 2 dramatically overhauled its news programs with a clearly
sensationalistic style both in form and in its coverage of stories.
Although local television news in Chicago certainly had toyed with
different sensationalistic devices prior to this time, the approach at
Channel 2 was in marked contrast to the approach previously
deemed acceptable. The move was carefully noted at the other news
competitors in the market, even those who were not direct competitors, like WGN-TV (which airs its newscasts at different times.) The
reactions at WGN-TV were interesting to note because they clearly
reflected differing perceptions of the audience, often reflective of
different organizational levels of news workers. Reporters and news
gatherers were more likely to voice criticism of the move, although
those working higher up on the organizational ladder were more
likely to show some appreciation for the move, perhaps cognizant of
stations' needs to fight the ratings war.

At WGN, the move was believed to reflect the concerns of news
management at WBBM-TV and its images of audience, in contrast
with the preferences of its own reporters. For example, WGN assignment manager Bernie Colleran describes his impression:

> The talk on the street is that the new man came in, saw that five
> stations in Chicago were essentially making the same news choices
> every day, and you can make a fairly good argument that he was damn
> well right. Saw that he was third in the O & O's (network owned and
> operated stations) in the ratings and didn't like being third and
> thought that "I've got to do something different, so I'm going to cover
> different stories," and he initially wasn't going to go too readily to the
> "John Calloway [Chicago public TV figure] type of tonight's issues in
> the news and what eggheads think what about issues in the news" so
> he went to top story, breaking story, gory story, more gory story.

Notice the view represented is that a new news director came to town, who, operating from an organizational vantage point, visualized the audience in terms of a ratings number that needed to be improved. The rationale for the move was clearly linked to those low ratings numbers. Predictably, that move was not well accepted by reporters at the CBS station (the occupational level most primarily concerned with story construction) according to WGN reporter Roseann Tellez:

> I know that [Channel 2] uses the consultants and the researchers to a much greater degree than we do. ... They take that stuff seriously. They use the research. You'll hear reporters complaining how the latest consultant came in and said, "No more stand-ups, standing still. Keep walking." Those types of suggestions carry over into what types of stories to cover and how to cover them.

Undoubtedly, Tellez is correct. When audience image is largely understood in terms of a ratings number, and increasing that number becomes the ultimate goal voiced at a news organization, that understanding does affect the types of stories that are covered and how they are covered. Tellez says she worked for a similarly sensationalistic station prior to her stint at WGN:

> It's happened to me before where I worked at a Gannett station where they took very seriously their research and the types of stories people wanted to see. They would analyze our numbers, determine what type of people watch our newscast, and make a grab for the people who didn't watch us. ... We would twist our focus to that group, trying to go for a larger audience.

During this study period, WGN-TV was clearly not as absorbed with its ratings numbers as the network owned-and-operated stations were. What was interesting, however, was WGN's preoccupation with WBBM's newscast. Almost every employee at WGN had a clear visceral reaction to the WBBM newscasts. Some talked with disdain about the approach, and others contended such an approach was overdue in the market. WGN executive producer, Tony Noce, was critical:

> They, right now, are going in for the spectacular: crime; very visual kinds of stories, whether they are local or not; any kind of train crash, plane crash, flood, even if it's way out anywhere ... that short attention span. I'm going to hit you with images very quickly just to keep you

focused, not so much understanding the story, but "just keeping you interested for the moment" kind of story.

The producer voices criticism of the newscasts at Channel 2 because they do not help the audience understand the news and the stories violate certain news values, such as proximity, " ... whether they are local or not ... even if it's way out anywhere." Although many at WGN voiced criticism of the approach at Channel 2, they also conceded that the new approach was doing some things right. Assistant news director Jim Disch focuses on writing:

> You don't want to become a Channel 2 because of a lot of the things that they are doing, but you can watch Channel 2 and you can pick out a few things ... that we should be doing better. ... I think they write a personal lead pretty well when they do it. I think it becomes a little bit laughable because they do it on every single story they write.

A second device Disch addresses is Channel 2's use of teases to promote upcoming stories in a newscast:

> I think they do a nice job teasing stories. The leads will break and they do a nice job of getting a nice cross-section of stories to keep you [tuned in]. I think they err in excess at times because what they will also do is tease the hell out of a story three times in the show and then try to satisfy your curiosity the last segment of the show with a 20-second clip or so.

Note that both issues Disch raised about Channel 2's coverage clearly pertain to their tactics that employ a clear marketing orientation to attract and maintain an audience—writing personal leads and teasing stories. Both devices are then criticized because of the extent to which they are overemployed at Channel 2. Disch seems to contend that the station has gone overboard in a marketing-orientation to the news, abandoning its professional values.

However, it is also at this occupational level (senior editors and news directors) that employees are likely to show appreciation for the move, likely because they are best tuned into organizational concerns to win an audience. For example, news director Paul Davis contends the approach at Channel 2 has affected all the news organizations in the Chicago market:

> I think the fact that [W]BBM was doing more tabloid was the cause of everybody to do a little more tabloid. We're trying to not do it like we

are doing it deliberately, taking that tact, and even so, the nights we lead with the ... murder of the woman in Skokie, we look a little like 2. So, I think we all kind of look like each other a little bit more. When somebody is doing something like bolder graphics, you'll see a little more, that kind of thing. One station's views of its audience has a broader impact than just the news it serves up to its audience. When the station is part of a competitive environment, it forces changes on all competing stations as well. Reporters and newsgatherers will more likely be critical of the move, although those higher up the organizational ladder will be more willing to accept the move as "part of the game." A new competitive approach to garner a higher audience share is just one more input into the social construction of news.

CONCLUSION

Different perspectives on the audience are inevitable in complex organizations because employees have differing goals. The news manager who is primarily interested in garnering higher ratings to enhance station profits will be more apt to perceive of the audience in terms of a market to be conquered. The assignment editor concerned with selecting news stories for coverage will grow to view the audience member as like himself, with the same interests and concerns. The reporter who is principally concerned with cranking out individual stories will more likely envision the audience in terms of the specific feedback to specific stories she hears from her sources on the street. None of the views, in and of themselves, are inaccurate. Those views, taken alone, are simply incomplete.

In the final chapter, my focus is on the news product that develops from the variety of views of the audience that are evidenced at news organizations. The best news products are believed to be those that are able to touch the audience in some special way.

Chapter 6

News to Touch the Audience

Audience images throughout the news organization are fundamental to the overall makeup of the news. Yet, those audience images are not always easy to assess, because much of journalists' and their news organizations' understanding of the audience are tacitly built into their everyday chores and functioning. In addition, journalists' individual understandings about the audience vary and are fragmented. Still, what these journalists perceive to be their best work is a news product that makes a special connection with their readers or viewers.

Journalists hope to make a difference. Their ultimate goal is to connect with their audience in such a way as to make some impact on them, to get them to see the world in a new light, to get them to understand a complex problem and make connections to their own lives, to get them to appreciate someone else's difficulties, to get them to laugh, to get them to take action. The goal is to involve the audience member in the news.

In this chapter, I review the role that journalists' and their organizations' perceptions of their audiences play in the construction of news. I begin by examining the basic conclusions that have theoretical implications for how news is constructed, arguing that audience cannot be neatly represented in models of the news process. I continue by considering the practical ways that news is produced, dependent on various perceptions of news readers or viewers. Specifically, in this section, I expand on notions presented in chapter 4 that point to the heightened news values of impact and interest. I argue that ultimately, journalists are seeking ways to touch their audience and make their writing empathetic. I conclude the chapter by discussing the future outlook for news organizations and their audiences.

AUDIENCE IN THE NEWS PRODUCT

Mass communication researchers who argue that journalists know little about their audience shortchange the impact that perceptions of the audience have on the news. Often, the problem is that researchers offer only a narrow definition of the audience. For example, Gans (1979) wrote: "I was surprised to find, however, that they [journalists] had little knowledge about their actual audience and rejected feedback from it" (p. 230). Such writing assumes that there is, indeed, one "actual audience" to which journalists could respond. As I suggested in previous chapters, audience (or, the actual audience) can be defined in any number of ways. It can refer to the audience member who calls in with a complaint, or it can refer to readers on the journalist's commute to work. To those who primarily view the news as a business, it might refer to the share of viewers who tune to a particular television newscast. To suggest that journalists don't know or respond to an actual audience assumes a narrow conception of audience. Although clearly there are individuals who watch a newscast or read a paper, it is not clear how they corporately form an actual audience.

Prior formalized models of the relation of the audience to the creation of news are oversimplified. For example, the basic communication model has been modified by a number of communication texts and simplified to look like that shown in Fig. 6.1.

When applied to news, the simple communication model suggests that the communication process involves a sender (the news organization) and the sending of a message (the news) over a channel

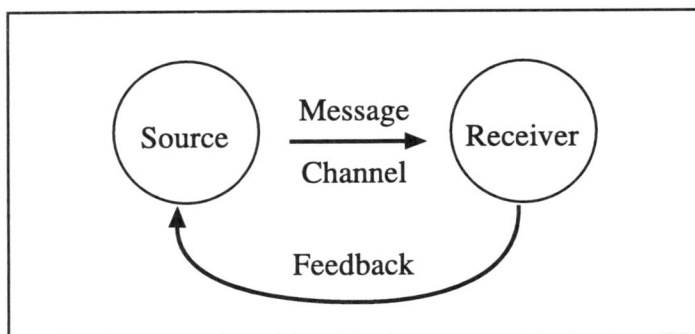

FIG. 6.1   Basic communication model.

(radio, TV waves, newspaper, etc.) to the receiver (targeted audience), with feedback (phone calls, letters, etc.) prompting the sender
to modify future news products. The natural implication of such a
model would be that journalists would be equally concerned with
creating messages for their news audience as they would be with
reacting to audience feedback. Such a conclusion simply does not
match up with journalists' description of their work. In addition,
simple notions of feedback from audience to source typically imply
some sort of intentional communication on the part of actual audience members. Much of the feedback from audience to source is
unintentional, such as that represented by the circulation figures of
a daily newspaper or by a journalist's observations on a train. The
simple feedback arrow says nothing about the imagery of the audience that is afforded the journalist or news organization. In addition,
feedback from audience to source bypasses a number of intervening
characteristics of the relationship between audience and the news-
makers. Such a model makes no distinction between working journalists and the organizations for whom they work. In addition, there
is no distinction between newsworkers at different levels within
news organizations. It is unrealistic to assume that workers at all
levels within the organization have the same goal: communicating
with an audience. As I illustrated in the last chapter, employees at
different organizational levels have different goals and different
conceptions of the audience.

In a model particularly focused on news construction, entitled
"The News Factory," Bantz, McCorcle, and Baade (1980) used the
news manufacturing metaphor to present a five-step "news factory
model" of the television newscast. Their model presents five stages
in the creation of the news: story ideation, task assignment, gathering and structuring materials, assembling materials, and last, presenting the newscast. Note that within their model, audience does
not appear to fit into the news factory equation at all.

Both models serve as metaphors for what really goes on in the
newsroom. Yet, they fail to address the complexity of the news
construction process and are unable to address the subtleties in the
way that audience becomes part of that process. Viewing newsmaking from a broader context, Ettema and Whitney (1994a) made such
a case in their critique of simplified models of communication:

A truly institutional conception of mass communication would not
deny, of course, that messages flow between communicators and receivers. Rather, it would subsume these flows, not merely into a
collection of signs that we call the "message," but into the vast

industrialized system of sign exchange for which DeFleur's box and arrows provided a rudimentary map. It would also subsume the connection between communicators and receivers, not merely into a "communication relationship," but into a process by which the "production subsystem" actively constructs and carefully maintains a network of relationships with, among others, that "taste-differentiated audience of consumers" (p. 4).

The interaction between audience inputs and the news process is complex and, therefore, does not fit neatly in any simple model of the communication process.

By and large, working journalists are concerned with what Ryan and Peterson (1982) labeled *product image* (pp. 24–25). That is, they are interested primarily in creating the news. It is imbedded in product image that we see assumptions about the audience. Notice how *Tribune* managing editor Dick Ciccone appeals to reporters' interest in their stories and those stories being disseminated to an audience in allaying reporters' fears about the future of the paper:

> I tell it to reporters: "What do you care whether 400,000 people read your story because they got it on a fax machine to take to the can or they get it at a big fat newspaper that they have to search through? As long as ... this company is disseminating to the people who want to take the time to understand it, that part of the mission is being fulfilled."

Although the reporter is keenly interested in producing stories, the reporter also has a secondary interest in the audience who reads them—a concern Ciccone addresses. Ciccone recognizes that reporters do want their material to reach a real audience and the interests of those audience members matter, not only to the individual reporters, but to the news organization as a whole. As case in point, Ciccone argues that the definition of news is changing, largely the result of technological changes that affect the audience:

> There is a very gray line about what is information and what is news today. ... I always thought the GNP [gross national product] figures were information. But now I think because of the society's different interests that they start to fall in the category of news. I think entertainment starts to fall into a gray line as well. If TCI [Telecommunications Inc.] and Southwest Bell and Paramount cut a deal (on a cable channel) that's going to run the same movie every 15 minutes all day ... well, is that entertainment or is that a news story?

Audience concerns help shape the definition of news in various ways that are not well suited to a simplified model of their impact on news construction. Reporters and news gatherers are most concerned with putting together news stories that make sense and that look polished. The tacit understanding is that those kinds of stories are the ones most likely to hold and maintain an audience. The better written story will be more intriguing to the reader, and the story with the best visuals will be more compelling to the viewer. Certainly, the reporter doesn't stop and make those mental assessments each time a story is produced. However, imbedded in the story production routine are the tacit understandings about the audience. Much of that understanding is developed within the process of day-in and day-out construction of the news—the process Schön referred to as knowing-in-action.

Editors and producers are most concerned with the look and content of the overall news product: the television show or the daily paper. Again, it is a rare moment when these workers stop to carefully consider their audience and its reactions to the overall news product, but audience considerations are still a very real part of product image. Whether the editor looks for a broad trend story or a groundbreaking story to grace the front page, or whether a producer looks to include three live shots during a noon newscast, tacit notions of the audience support those decisions whether or not they are part of the conscious decision-making process. Implicitly, the editor works on the assumption that either the audience needs a trend story that will tie into their personal lives or a groundbreaking story that will grab their attention on the front page of the paper. The producer who is proud of the fact that he is able to incorporate three live shots in the newscast works on the tacit assumption that viewers are compelled by things that happen *as* they happen.

Senior editors, producers, and news directors are best able to understand the role of their news products in the array of materials offered by their parent company. From their perspective, the role of the news is to make money. A news show makes money when it garners high ratings and is an attractive purchase for advertisers. A newspaper makes money when it is packaged and zoned to achieve big circulation figures. When a newspaper editor takes pride in the level of zoning used at the paper, he or she works with the tacit understanding that readers are more interested in what happens in their own backyard than they are in the goings-on in city government. When a news director makes a decision about whether his or her news team can afford to send a reporter to the state capital and uplink a story back to his market, he or she works with the tacit assumption that such a story would be valuable to his or her viewers and (when promoted properly) might pay for itself in additional ratings points.

THE NATURE OF NEWS

What Schudson (1989) labeled the "sociology of news production" (p. 263) presumes that news is a *constructed reality* (Tuchman, 1978). One important source of that social construction among newsworkers and news organizations are images of the audience. It is part of the "practical accomplishment" that puts the news together. One way audience imagery helps define and determine what constitutes the news is by the way it shapes news factors.

News factors are characteristics traditionally used to help define news. According to Itule and Anderson (1987), news is thought to be timely, proximate, prominent, of conflict, of consequence, and of interest. Although professional journalists rarely string these thoughts together in deciding if a piece merits coverage, they do often resort to these ideals in trying to describe what they do and how they do it. Journalism students are trained to use these criteria in determining what is and what is not news.

Although news factors help to offer an official description of what constitutes news, they also help to routinize news production by implying that news should be covered in a particular way. For instance, by arguing that live news reports are the most timely and, therefore, some of the most important stories for the audience, the news factor of timeliness dictates that live shots are to be an essential component of the broadcast news show.

Those news factors have imbedded within them a particular notion of the audience. For instance, to argue that news must be timely suggests that the news audience has a strong appetite for knowing the latest details in a breaking story and quickly tires of "old" news. It suggests an active, or perhaps a "hyperactive," audience that is more concerned with recency than with depth and understanding. News factors become part of the tacit understanding about what is covered and how it is covered. Implied within those tacit news factors are even more tacit assumptions about the audience.

Girding the news factors are the journalists' and their organizations' dual concerns for winning and maintaining an audience and their professional values, which dictate that important information is disseminated. Therefore, the ultimate goal for journalists at both news organizations observed seems to be to somehow mix the important with the interesting, so as to both engage and touch the audience member, that is, have real impact. WGN news director Paul Sanders says the key is touching the viewer's emotions:

> If we were to determine that you needed to know about something, and we produced a story about it, and you were bored by it, ... then ... either we didn't produce it very well, or we were wrong. If we do that kind of work and it goes right past you, ... then we have forgotten the old factors and rules. We failed to attach an emotional tendril to it to show you why this is interesting to you.

Tribune metro editor Jean Davidson also points to emotion as a key that can make the important story interesting. Emotion engages the readers, drawing them into the story. She also argues that a key is to demonstrate personal relevance to the reader, to show how the story might affect them:

> There is an emotional element. That is certainly one. We're working on a story now about a 6-year-old boy who brought a gun to school. And this was a little blip on the radar screen. It didn't get much attention this week, and we're trying to explore the layers of that story. Why it happened. It happened in the Austin neighborhood—a bad neighborhood. But this was a kid who had never been threatened himself, and his family had never had violent experiences. So maybe it could have happened in Naperville or Arlington Heights [affluent suburban areas] too.

Beyond broadening a story to show that it applies to a number of people, journalists at both news organizations try to make important stories interesting by working toward making their stories empathetic, akin to something Schwartz (1974) called, "striking a responsive chord." Although Schwartz wrote about advertising, the concept applies to these journalists as well:

> The critical task is to design our package of stimuli so that it resonates with information already stored within an individual and thereby induces the desired learning or behavioral effect. Resonance takes place when the stimuli put into our communication evoke meaning in a listener or viewer. That which we put into the communication has no meaning in itself. The meaning of our communication is what a listener or viewer gets out of his experience with the communicator's stimuli. (pp. 24–25)

Schwartz's writings suggest that the goal of the communicator is largely enthematic—providing the essential information and allowing the audience to fill in the syllogism. For the journalist, this seems to translate into basic messages, such as "There are social evils in the world." The audience member can be left to deduce that his or her personal involvement is necessary to right these wrongs. Another message the journalist might convey is that an innocent boy was shot to death while walking to school. Audience members are left to conclude that then they are vulnerable too. Or, the suburban reader might be left to conclude that the city is a dangerous place, but thankfully, the suburbs are a safe haven (or, perhaps not!).

A number of the stories these journalists are most proud of seek to strike this responsive chord with their audience. The goal is to elicit empathy with the audience member. The enthematic message may be nothing more than having the audience member ask, "Gee, how would I feel if that were me?" It seems to be a key factor in making some stories more compelling than others. An important story gains coverage because it makes a special kind of impact on its audience—it elicits empathy. Stories like this draw the viewer into them. The *Tribune*'s "Killing Our Children" series tends to do this. Even the feature's name calls on the reader to identify with the story. It is entitled, "Killing *Our* Children" rather than "Killing *the* Children." The reader is called on to take claim to these kids. A front-page headline of the series is featured on March 3. It reads "Why him? Why 17 wounds?" (Kiernan, 1993, p. 1). The title asks the reader to try to make sense of the senseless, just as those in the youth's immediate community must address the same questions. The story's lead further draws the reader into the boy's life and death by describing minor, but intimate details of the youth's life:

Whenever his stepfather worked on the television sets and VCRs he repairs for a living, James Nance watched intently.

He never said a word, never asked to help. He just watched with the intense gaze and slight smile that was his customary expression.

Then, one night in January, Joe Hart and Ella Nance came home to find a sheepish James surrounded by a pile of wires and other pieces of a television he had taken apart and was able to put back together.

Now, it is the pieces of his life that lie exposed and in disarray, scattered about for those who knew him to puzzle over and to try to make sense of.

When he was killed on the corner of 50th and Elizabeth Streets on Sunday night, James left behind a body pierced with 17 bullet wounds and a tangle of questions about why someone would have wanted to murder a 13-year-old boy saying goodnight to his girlfriend.

The writer made the *important* story *interesting* by creating a special kind of *impact*. He forced the reader to enter into the story. Next to the story is a box with a graphic that reads, "Seven dead in 1993." Under the heading, "Killing Our Children" a brief description reads, "Changed behavior and gaps in school attendance marked the last days of James Nance, the latest Chicago-area child under 15 [killed] this year."

Two pictures accompany the story, one of Nance prior to his death and another of his friend after the shooting. That caption reads, "'It's scary to know someone who has been shot,' says Chris Mason, 12, of his friend and neighbor, James Nance, 13."

The overall coverage begs the reader to become part of the story, to wrestle with the moral questions, to grieve the lost child. By drawing the reader into the story, it is able to effectively interest and engage the reader. Certainly, parents can identify with the pride of Nance's parents when they discovered his ability to put together a television set, just like his stepfather. And certainly they can identify with the pain such a loss might bring.

Tribune metro Editor Jean Davidson explains it this way:

> As a reporter, on the street I covered all this mayhem and the stories … many of them didn't affect me personally until I talked to relatives, someone who truly personally felt the loss, and then you can't help but feel it. So, I think that we need to stress empathy in our writing about all those kinds of stories, and we need to train aspiring journalists to deal with those situations. … I have two daughters, and I know that since I became a mother, I am personally affected much, much more than I ever was before if I read about a child abuse case or child that was killed. It often can bring tears to my eyes, and I was hardened, I thought.

When a story can bring tears to a reader's eyes, it is clearly making an impact on the reader. Journalists' descriptions of their goals suggest they want their coverage to go beyond simple interest. WGN assignment editor Mike Kertez talks about his goals for his newscast:

> I'd like people to be turned on by the news, to be interested in the person they saw on the show, and to think they had some picture of what was happening that day, … that it appealed to everything they

do so they could use their mind to understand the story ... rather than just watch it, ... that every part of what they understand about life is being helped.

Rather than his viewers just watching a story, Kertez hopes they will use their own minds to work through what they are seeing, to become part of the story. He is hoping his news will strike a responsive chord. Schwartz (1974) wrote:

> The communicator must be aware of the attachments people will make between his stimuli and their previous experiences. The accuracy or reality of our stimuli is often less important in determining their ultimate meaning than the pattern listeners will apply in making sense of something they hear. (p. 33)

Although these journalists would not readily agree that their accurate portrayal of reality has a lessor importance, some discussions suggest they do recognize that their job is to try to trigger some already existing emotions and experiences of their audience. *Tribune* photo assignment editor Frank Hames talks about the focus of some of his paper's pictures:

> It doesn't necessarily have to be someone hanging out a window, or if it's a big enough fire and there is enough damage, we can just show the amount of fire there is or show a fireman that is really working hard or something like that or ... somebody on the roof tops to show something with emotion.

WGN news director Paul Davis contends there are key emotions that stories must touch if they are to be effective in reaching the viewer:

> You can look at the Mowrer [1960] learning theory in which he said our intelligence cannot be awakened, as it were, without emotional triggers ... and I translate it to our business. You have to get the emotional attention with either fear or hope, relief or disappointment in your story as the receiver would view the information. ... Absent any of those four pieces of emotional baggage, you won't get anything.

Although most journalists may not have such a calculated sense of the need to touch a key emotion, they do seek to make their stories come alive for their audience—to have a special kind of impact. In his text *The Power of News,* Schudson (1995) wrote, "good journalism often is the means by which empathy is evoked" (p. 8). One such effort is displayed in the work of *Tribune* reporter Andy Fagelman. After a court proceeding one day in which a woman with AIDS sought to have her sister named guardian once she became incapacitated, Fagelman unsuccessfully attempted to interview the woman. He explains the value of such an interview:

> Just to put a human face on the situation. We know that this is something that has a lot of significance beyond just her individual case. ... You hear so much about AIDS, but it's sort of just numbers, and you don't really get a sense of the people behind the numbers, and I think it gives you a little more understanding of what somebody's going through.

By getting the interview with the woman, Fagelman would hope to make a special impact on the lives of his readers—to give them a sense of the frustration and pain experienced by the AIDS victim. Metro editor Jean Davidson uses the word *engaging* to describe a front-page story on February 25 that was written in a way to draw a connection between the reader and the subject of the piece. The story, authored by reporter Terry Wilson (1993), is titled "Only the Victim Has a Life Sentence":

> Jose Roman's family wheeled him into Juvenile court recently so a teenager who conspired to blast Roman's brain with a shotgun could see what he had done.
>
> The 16-year-old gang member apparently couldn't face the sight. He kept his head down, his eyes averted from the wheelchair.
>
> There Roman, 21, sat wrapped in a blanket, awake but unaware of his surroundings, unable to speak, move or eat.
>
> Less than a year ago he was a strong, healthy young father of two small children who hoped to become an auto mechanic.
>
> Then last March he was walking home from a friend's house, listening to music on headphones, when he was mistaken for a gang member and shot by members of another gang. ...
>
> "I did want him to see the damage he did," Cathy Roman, Roman's 22-year-old sister said of the teenager in court. "It would be good if he could have nightmares like we do." (News Section, p. 1)

If the story works in drawing a connection among the reader, reporter, and the victim's family, it is perhaps because it has been crafted in such a way so as to force the reader to stand in the shoes of those being portrayed in the story. Details are provided that draw a natural link between victim and reader. The victim walked home wearing headphones, like many people do. The victim had simple manageable goals: to become an auto mechanic. The victim had a sister about his age, and he had two small children. He sounded like just about anyone and everyone. Readers are forced to recognize themselves in the story. They come to identify with the details of the story. The enthematic message is that if this could happen to someone innocently walking home from a friend's house, it could just as easily happen to me or my friends. The responsive chord has been sounded. The editor suggests why she thinks the story worked:

> It wouldn't have been on page 1 except for the fact that the reporter did such a good job of bringing home the point that not only this man, Jose Roman, is so debilitated and will never be the same, even though the guy who shot him will be out in two or three years, but she just painted a portrait of all the caring in that family. And it just was a wonderful very well-rounded story; it's not one-dimensional and it is a story that I think that I read and a lot of other people read even though we've read a lot of awful crime and maiming stories. This one was different because it had all those elements that gave it great depth.

The story's ability to graphically touch readers' emotions is an example of sounding the responsive chord. For reporters and editors at these two news organizations, the highest form of newstelling is that which is able to make an impact on the audience in a special way. This kind of impact is the result of a synergy between the important story and the interesting angle. The remote news story is brought home to the readers or viewers in a way that calls on them to be part of the story. This special kind of impact calls on the audience members to identify with the characters and engage the situation on some personal level. Establishing this kind of impact becomes the device for making important stories interesting. For reporters, it translates into a higher calling than their traditional adherence to precepts of objectivity, which call for a more detached stance in their reporting. It is calling the journalists to take a special involvement in their reporting and to get their audience to do so as well.

NEWS AND AUDIENCES OF THE FUTURE

One of the most clear trends voiced by media prognosticators on the relationship between news organizations and their future audiences is that audience members are expected to take a greater role in selecting the news they see and to possess the ability to tailor the news product to meet their individual needs. Such a view is clearly evidenced at these Tribune Company news organizations. *The Chicago Tribune* continues to increase its focus on more narrow zoning of its newspaper. The paper is also looking for ways to allow its readers the chance to pick out the parts of the paper they want to read. Online computer technologies are clearly a likelihood for disseminating the paper of the future, according to managing editor Dick Ciccone:

> Much of what we do is [provide] information that someday someone else will make available far easier, far more accessible. Maybe it will be *The Chicago Tribune,* but certainly we're not forever going to keep chopping down trees to print eight pages of NASDAQ and mutual funds. ... Clearly there are going to be much easier ways to access that information in the future, whether it's fiber optics and cable supplied by a technical company with information provided by an information-gathering company like *The Chicago Tribune.* ... Clearly, the easiest way in the future to deliver classified ads [is by online searches].

Ciccone envisions a more dynamic relationship between the reader and the newspaper of the future, one based largely on technological advances:

> Dow Jones has a theory that works for their readers and their advertisers. They tell their advertisers, "We will get your message to whomever you want however you want to get it to them" and to their readers, "We will get you your information whenever you want it, however you want it. You want it in the newspaper? Do you want it by fiber optics on your TV screen? Do you want it by fax? Do you want it by direct mail?"

Ciccone envisions a world of much more interactivity among newspaper, advertiser, and reader in the future. He speculates that in 20 years, the paper could be delivered by fax and would only be 20 pages in length. In addition, readers would have access to all sorts of other information, such as specific stock quotations. Clearly, much of the technology Ciccone envisions is already possible. He acknowledges that the paper can already be accessed each morning by Chicago Online. Technology has also been changing the news outlook of broadcast organizations. For example, it is now commonplace for television stations to provide live remote news reports from locations far outside their immediate viewing area. And staff members at WGN recognize that as technology advances, so do the expectations of the viewing audience. Writer Tim Jackson contends that his audience is now more interested in stories far outside their home:

> We're much more globally attainable. In fact, we ran a story last night that Motorola is developing a new global outreach instantaneous telephone contact kind of number. I'm not even sure I understand how it works. But it's going to be yet another barrier that's come down. ... And I think that really changes the focus of how people learn about news and information. It therefore changes the focus of what's important. 'Cause they're now getting information all day long. ... Now they can watch news all day and all night long almost anywhere they are in the world and, with either a phone or television or satellite dish or a pocket computer, they're going to be able to get a lot of information. They can now.

Advances in technology change the way news can be disseminated, which changes the way audience members can receive the news. That has an impact on which information is deemed important.

Beyond WGN and *The Chicago Tribune,* it is clear that the Tribune Company is making changes in response to changes in technology and therefore changes in its prospective audience. For example, in a business story dated July 7 (Widder, 1993), *The Chicago Tribune* reported about its parent company:

> Tribune Co. sent another signal Tuesday that it intends to be a player in tomorrow's multimedia world of information delivery by announcing two acquisitions that are relatively small in size but large in potential.
>
> The company is buying Compton's Multimedia Publishing Group from Chicago-based Encyclopedia Britannica Inc. for $57 million in cash, and Contemporary Books Inc., a non-fiction publisher, for $40 million in cash and Tribune stock. Both firms are privately held.
>
> ... This acquisition continues Tribune's recent forays into new delivery systems. The company has invested in StarSight Telecast, an on-screen electronic bulletin board service for consumers (an investment that allowed creation of Chicago Online, which features elec-

tronic distribution of the Chicago Tribune); and Picture Network International, an on-line photo archive. The company also is a sponsor of the News of the Future project at the Massachusetts Institute of Technology's MediaLab. (Business Section, p. 1)

News employees like Ciccone and Jackson envision a more active audience member of the future, one who will be equipped and interested in accessing targeted bits of information. In addition, the Tribune Company is also readying itself for such a world. Such a technological focus may be a bit overly optimistic about the television viewer and newspaper reader if Neuman's (1991) projections are true:

> Those with the ability and inclination to become scholarly geniuses have done so throughout history. Where once they used telescopes, libraries, typewriters, and slide rules, they now may turn to computers. But they represent only a tiny fraction of the mass population. In the language of the industry, they compose a very small market. They may be important to society, but not to the marketplace. The future of the mass audience will pivot on factors of mass psychology and market economics. (p. 78)

Both of those forces, Neuman (1991) contends, will retard the use that modern mass audiences will make of the new technologies and slow the growth of the new technologies into the market. Yet, despite Neuman's analysis, individuals in communications companies are assuming that audiences are indeed changing in reaction to the more sophisticated technologies that enable them to access more personalized information. The current popularity of news resources on the Internet seems to bear out the wisdom of those assumptions. Both Tribune organizations have their eye on the future and on a changing audience.

CONCLUSION

If one assumes that news is a social construction that evolves out of a myriad of inputs and exigencies, it is logical to assume that one of those key inputs are newsworkers' perceptions of their audience. Whether individual journalists have a clear understanding about the demographics or psychographics of their audience or whether they envision their audience as simply those with whom they come in contact during an individual week, those perceptions can and do have a potent effect on the news that is eventually produced. For example, direct contact with audience members through letters and phone calls has been shown to produce changes from even the highest levels of the newsrooms, albeit, they are, typically, stylistic changes.

Still, the relation between perceptions of the audience by news workers and the news product they make is not direct. Professional values are still a very real part of the makeup of these individual journalists and the organizations for whom they work. Such values tend to dictate that journalists ought to be the ones to tell their audience which stories are important, indeed, which stories ought to be considered news. Tacit understandings about the audience that stem from what Schön called knowing-in-action and broader philosophical understandings that stem from what Schön called reflecting-in-action also affect the content and shape of the news. Such understandings heighten the rank of certain news values, such as interest and impact, and reduce the rank of others including proximity, prominence, and so forth.

Traditional news values are imbedded with notions of the audience. For example, proximity suggests an audience with parochial concerns, who are more likely to be interested in events in their own neighborhoods than in events across the planet. The most important news values for these journalists appear to be those that are most clearly linked to the audience—interest and impact.

Journalists at the two Chicago news organizations observed in this study see their best work as those stories that are able to demonstrate that they have impact on their audience. Impact is the key device by which journalists are able to tie audience interest to what they deem to be important for their audience. This special kind of impact is also the result of a synergy between journalists' important stories and the interesting angles used to tell them. The best news stories, as judged by news workers in these organizations, are those that are able to poignantly touch audience members and elicit empathy, striking a responsive chord.

Ultimately, journalists and the organizations for which they work focus on producing news products, be they stories or newspapers or newscasts as a whole. By examining those news texts and the understandings of those who produce them, the communication researcher can learn a great deal about the explicit and implicit understandings of the audience that contribute to the construction of those news texts.

References

Akhavan-Majid, R., & Wolf, G. (1991). American mass media and the myth of libertarianism: Toward an "elite power group" theory. *Critical Studies in Mass Communication, 8,* 139–151.

Ang, I. (1991). *Desperately seeking the audience.* London: Routledge.

Bantz, C. R., McCorcle, S., & Baade, R. (1980). The news factory. *Communication Research, 7(1),* 45–68.

Berkowitz, D. (1992). Non-routine news and newswork: Exploring a what-a-story. *Journal of Communication, 42,* 82–94.

Berkowitz, D., & Beach, D. W. (1993). News sources and news content: The effect of routine news, conflict and proximity. *Journalism Quarterly, 70,* 4–12.

Biagi, S. (1987). *NewsTalk II: State-of-the art conversations with today's broadcast journalists.* Belmont, CA: Wadsworth.

Brooks, B. S., Kennedy, G., Moen, D. R., & Ranley D. (1988). *News reporting and writing.* New York: St. Martin's Press.

Carey, J. W. (1986). Why and how: The dark continent of American journalism. In R. K. Manoff & M. Schudson (Eds.), *Reading the news* (pp. 146–196). New York: Pantheon.

Chang, T. K., & Kraus, S. (1990). News for the other person: Editors' processing of readers' interest. In S. Kraus (Ed.), *Mass communication and political information processing* (pp. 99–112). Hillsdale, NJ: Lawrence Erlbaum Associates.

Charnley, M. V. (1975). *Reporting* (3rd ed.). New York: Holt, Rinehart & Winston.

Darnton, R. (1990). *The kiss of the Lamourette: Reflections in cultural history.* New York: Norton.

Dennis, E. E., & Merrill, J. C. (1984). *Basic issues in mass communication.* New York: Macmillan.

Dimmick, J. (1974). The Gate Keeper: An uncertainty theory. *Journalism Monographs, 37.*

Emery, E., & Emery, M. (1988). *The press and America: An interpretative history of the mass media* (6th ed.). Englewood Cliffs, NJ: Prentice-Hall.

Espinosa, P. (1982). The audience in the text: Ethnographic observations of a Hollywood story conference. *Media, Culture and Society, 4,* 77–86.

Ettema, J. S. (1988). The craft of the investigative journalist. *Research Monograph of the Institute for Modern Communications.* Evanston, IL: Northwestern University.

Ettema, J. S., & Whitney, D. C. (1994a). The money arrow: An introduction to audience-making. In J. S. Ettema & D. C. Whitney (Eds.), *Audiencemaking: Media audiences as industrial process* (pp. 1–18). Newbury Park, CA: Sage.

Ettema, J. S., & Whitney, D. C. (1994b, July). *Professional mass communicators and their organizations.* Paper presented at the International Communication Association Convention, Sydney, Australia.

Ettema, J. S., & Whitney, D. C. (Eds.). (1994c). *Audiencemaking: Media audiences as industrial process.* Newbury Park, CA: Sage.

Fishman, M. (1980). *Manufacturing the news.* Austin: University of Texas Press.

Fishman, M. (1982). News and nonevents: Making the visible invisible. In J. S. Ettema & D. C. Whitney (Eds.), *Individuals in mass media organizations: Creativity and constraint* (pp. 219–240). Beverly Hills, CA: Sage.

Flegel, R. C., & Chaffee, S. H. (1971). Influences of editors, readers and personal opinions on reporters. *Journalism Quarterly, 48,* 645–51.

Gamson, W. A. (1984). *What's news: A game simulation of TV news.* New York: Free Press.

Gans, H. J. (1979). *Deciding what's news: A study of CBS Evening News, NBC Nightly News, Newsweek and Time.* New York: Pantheon.

Gaunt, P. (1990). *Choosing the news: The profit factor in news selection.* New York: Greenwood.

Goering, L. (1993, February 21). Few know it but it's back to polls Tuesday. *The Chicago Tribune,* News Section, p. 1.

Hackett, R. A. (1984). Decline of a paradigm: Bias and objectivity in news media studies. *Critical Studies in Mass Communication, 1,* 229–259.

Hallin, D. C. (1992). The passing of the "high modernism" of American journalism. *Journal of Communication, 42,* 14–25.

Hirsch, P. M. (1977). Occupational, organizational, and institutional models in mass media research: Toward an integrated framework. In P. M. Hirsch, P. V. Miller, & F. G. Kline (Eds.), *Strategies for communication research* (Vol. 6, pp. 13–42). Beverly Hills, CA: Sage.

Hohenberg, J. (1960). *The professional journalist.* New York: Henry Holt & Company.

Hough, G. A. (1995). *News writing* (5th ed.). Boston: Houghton Mifflin.

Itule, B. D., & Anderson, D. A. (1987). *News writing and reporting for today's media.* New York: Random House.

Izard, R. I., Culbertson, H. M., & Lambert, D. A. (1990). *Fundamentals of news reporting* (5th ed.). Dubuque, IA: Kendall/Hunt.

Kaniss, P. (1991). *Making local news.* Chicago: The University of Chicago Press.

Kennedy, G., Moen, D. R., & Ranly, D. (1993). *Beyond the inverted pyramid: Effective writing for newspapers, magazines and specialized publications.* New York: St. Martin's Press.

Kiernan, L. (1993, March 3). Why him? Why 17 wounds? *The Chicago Tribune,* New Section, p. 1.

Lavine, J. M., & Wackman, D. B. (1988). *Managing media organizations.* New York: Longman.

Mayer, M. (1993). *Making news* (2nd ed.). Boston: Harvard Business School Press.

McQuail, D., (1983). *Mass communication theory: An introduction.* London: Sage.

Mencher, M. (1981). *News reporting and writing* (2nd ed.). Dubuque, IA: Brown.

Mencher, M. (1994). *News reporting and writing* (6th ed.). Madison, WI, and Dubuque, IA: Brown and Benchmark.

Miller, S. (1992, September). Reaching readers of the future: Who will our readers be? What will they want? *Quill, 80,* 30–31.

Minow, N. (1961, May). *Program control: The broadcasters are public trustees.* Speech presented at the National Association of Broadcasters Annual Convention, Washington, DC.

Morton, L. P., & Warren, J. (1992). Proximity: Localization vs. distance in PR news releases. *Journalism Quarterly, 69,* 102–1028.

Mowrer, O. H. (1960). *Learning theory and the symbolic processes.* New York: Wiley.

Neuman, W. R. (1991). *The future of the mass audience.* Cambridge, England: Cambridge University Press.

Owen B. W., & Wildman, S. S. (1992). *Video economics.* Cambridge, MA: Harvard University Press.

Pearson, R. (1993, March 4). Edgar throws down gauntlet, foes run with it. *The Chicago Tribune,* News Section, p. 1.

Polanyi, M. (1966). *The tacit dimension.* Garden City, NY: Doubleday.

Pool, I., & Shulman, I. (1959). Newsmen's fantasies, audiences, and newswriting. *Public Opinion Quarterly, 23,* 145–158.

Quigley, L. (1959). *The blind men and the elephant.* New York: Charles Scribner's Sons.

Recktenwald, W. (1992, November 11). One man suffers, we all pay. *The Chicago Tribune,* News Section, p. 1.

Recktenwald, W. (1993, April 16). Cop promotion logjam may end. *The Chicago Tribune,* Chicagoland Section, p. 1.

Ryan, J., & Peterson, R. A. (1982). The product image: The fate of creativity in country music songwriting. In J. S. Ettema & D. C. Whitney (Eds.), *Individuals in mass media organizations: Creativity and constraint* (pp. 11–32). Beverly Hills, CA: Sage.

Schlesinger, P. (1978). *Putting "reality" together.* London: Constable & Company.

Schön, D. A. (1983). *The reflective practitioner: How professionals think in action.* New York: Basic Books.

Schudson, M. (1986). When: Deadlines, datelines, and history. In R. K. Manoff & M. Schudson (Eds.), *Reading the news* (pp. 79–108). New York: Pantheon.

Schudson, M. (1989). The sociology of news production. In *Media, culture and society* (Vol. 11, pp. 263–282). London: Sage.

Schudson, M. (1995). *The power of news.* Cambridge, MA: Harvard.

Schwartz, T. (1974). *The responsive chord.* Garden City, NY: Doubleday.

Siebert, F. S., Peterson, T., & Schramm, W. (1956). *Four theories of the press.* Urbana: University of Illinois Press.

Smith, M. P. (1992, September). Think globally, edit locally. *Quill,* 34– 36.

Squires, J. D. (1993). *Read all about it: The corporate takeover of America's newspapers.* New York: Random House.

Stone, G. (1987). *Examining newspapers: What research reveals about America's newspapers.* Newbury Park, CA: Sage.

Strentz, H. (1989). *News reporters and news sources: Accomplices in shaping and misshaping the news* (2nd ed.). Ames: Iowa State University Press.

Tribune Company. (1992). "My choice?" *Tribune* [1992 annual report]. Chicago: Author.

Tuchman, G. (1978). *Making news.* New York: Free Press.

Weaver, D. H., & Wilhoit, G. C. (1986). *The American journalist.* Bloomington: Indiana University Press.

Webster, J. G., & Phalen, P. (1994). Audience models in communication policy. In J. S. Ettema & D. C. Whitney (Eds.), *Audiencemaking: Media audiences as industrial process* (pp. 19–37). Newbury Park, CA: Sage.

White, D. M. (1950). The "Gate Keeper": A case study in the selection of news. *Journalism Quarterly, 27,* 383–390.

Whitney, D. C., & Ettema, J. S. (1991, May). *Raising the level of analysis in media-audience studies.* Paper presented at the International Communication Association Convention, Chicago.

Widder, P. (1993, July 7). *Tribune* buys Multimedia, book firms. *The Chicago Tribune,* Business Section, p. 1.

Wilson, T. (1993, February 25). Only the victim has a life sentence. *The Chicago Tribune,* News Section, p. 1.

Wuliger, G. T. (1991). The moral universes of libertarian press theory. *Critical Studies in Mass Communication, 8,* 152–167.

Yoakam, R. D., & Cremer, C. F. (1989). *ENG: Television news and the new technology (2nd ed.).* New York: Random House.

Author Index

Subject Index

About the Author

Dwight DeWerth-Pallmeyer is an assistant professor of journalism at California Polytechnic State University. He joined the faculty in the Fall of 1996 and is faculty advisor of the campus radio station. DeWerth-Pallmeyer formerly taught in the Departments of Speech at Utica College of Syracuse University and at Augustana College in Rock Island, Illinois. He was faculty advisor of the campus radio stations at both colleges. He has also served as News Director at Public Radio, WVIK in Rock Island, Illinois, and at CBS-affiliate KOJO in Laramie, Wyoming.

DeWerth-Pallmeyer grew up in St. Louis, Missouri. He holds a BA in journalism from Valparaiso University, Valparaiso, Indiana, an MA in Mass Communication from the University of Minnesota, and a PhD in Communication Studies from Northwestern University. He is married to Amy DeWerth-Pallmeyer and has one daughter, Rachel. The family lives near San Luis Obispo, California.